POETRY MATTERS

Edited by Helen Davies & Donna Samworth

The Midlands

First published in Great Britain in 2011 by:

 Young**Writers**

Remus House
Coltsfoot Drive
Peterborough
PE2 9BF
Telephone: 01733 890066
Website: www.youngwriters.co.uk

Foreword

Since our inception in 1991, Young Writers has endeavoured
to promote poetry and creative writing within schools by
running annual nationwide competitions. These competitions
are designed to develop and nurture the burgeoning creativity
of the next generation, and give them valuable confidence in
their own abilities.

This regional anthology is one of the series produced by our
latest secondary school competition, *Poetry Matters*.
Using poetry as their tool, the young writers were given the
opportunity to tell the world what matters to them. The authors
of our favourite three poems were also given the chance to
appear on the front cover of their region's collection.

Whilst skilfully conveying their opinions through poetry, the
writers showcased in this collection have simultaneously
managed to give poetry a breath of fresh air, brought it to life
and made it relevant to them. Using a variety of themes and
styles, our featured poets leave a lasting impression of their
inner thoughts and feelings, making this anthology a rare
insight into the next generation.

Contents

The Poems

You Are Nothing But Sadly Mistaken

He knows you've lived your life
And you understand that it's his turn to outgrow Pooh?
And he knows you've made mistakes,
But you know they're not his, don't you?

He's meant to be the smart one,
But is shown no respect?
He's meant to be most mature,
But hasn't earned trust yet?

He knows he can make mistakes,
But they're not anything like yours.
So don't tell him that you know,
When you are in fact the cause.

I know it sounds clichéd,
The whole teenage: *you don't understand!*
But the fact of the matter is . . . you don't.
You don't live inside my mind.
You don't know what I think.
You don't understand my actions.
Let alone the reasoning as to why I do them.

So next time, take a step back
And think about what he did.
Don't stand there and tell him it's all wrong,
After all . . . he's just a kid.

You were born with ears, were you not?
And yet you are as uninformed as a child that's been taken.
Arguments caused by issues that were never there?
My apologies. But you're nothing but sadly mistaken.

Sian Hancock (14)
Abraham Darby Academy, Telford

The Time Has Come . . .

The time has come, September already
Secondary school - I'll take it steady.

Nervous and excited at the building and
Place - where do I go? I really don't know.

The bell, it rings, we're all in tow,
Time for mentor, off I go . . .

Registration is called, 'Here Sir,' I reply -
A smile of joy, in return I wanna cry.

We're called to the hall for a talk - I know
Mr Hawke, his name - expectations, he wants to grow!

A cheerful man makes it easier for me,
No more worries let's wait and see!

The bell rings for Ash -
Time for food at last -
Something hot, something cold,
What shall I have? I can't be told.

I explore the grounds of the time I have left -
To gather my thoughts of the day I've had,
I keep walking and thinking of all that's gone on —
Not bad - after all - it's really fun!

Rush, rush, the bell rings again,
Off to maths, I'll do it all again.

What a fantastic day after all -
Nothing to worry, Year 7 is all a ball!

Abbie Brown (11)
Abraham Darby Academy, Telford

I Want To Be A . . .

I want to be a singer,
So I can sing and get a good wage.
I want to be an artist
So I can paint with the colour beige.

I want to be a dancer,
So I can show my moves and shake.
I want to be a baker,
So I can bake a chocolate cake.

I want to be a hairdresser,
So I can style people's hair.
I want to be a hunter,
So I can catch a massive bear.

I want to be a milkman,
So I can deliver all the milk.
I want to be a designer,
So I can sew a dress out of silk.

Nerys Howes (11)
Abraham Darby Academy, Telford

The Final Curtain Call

Standing in the wings,
Nervous and all a-quiver,
I can hear the audience talking,
Which makes my legs *shiver!*

I start walking forward,
I find myself on stage,
My heart misses a beat
And I hope I do amaze.

The final curtain call,
The audience cheer and shout,
I get a bouquet of flowers,
What a great night out!

Alicia Bennett (11)
Abraham Darby Academy, Telford

Pets

Long, short, straight, flat; these are the hairs upon my cat.
Dirty, messy, sleeps like a log; these are the qualities of my dog.
Slithers, creeps, coils around the rake; these are the movements of my snake.
Burrows, digs, eats carrots as a habit; this is the lifestyle of my rabbit.
Green, brown, orange and fudgey; these are the colours of my budgie.
Spending, lending, getting in debt; these are the consequences of my pets!

Conrad Carrolan (15)
Ashby School, Ashby de la Zouch

Paper Epitaph

You were a leech, soulless and pinned beneath
That tyrant's thumb, stepdad who clamped your tongue,
Stepdad whose castle rotted, whose right was wrong.

The bouncing, pride-sick rat's incessant shriek
Was yours after you bruised a brace of flowers.
You could not love life, colour, scent or taste
So each apple became a cart of sours.

In times to be forgotten I saved you.
News reached me of light fittings, ropes and knives.
Adhesives tore your fragile heart asunder,
I cared: your only gratitude was lies,

Jealousy; round my love, a cloud of flies.
So forgive me for flying off the handle
When your vile cavern spewed forth acid words.

Justice is done. You will not breed
You will not breed, you will not breed.
Ideas will not diffuse into our minds.
This race won't have your seed. This race will live,

Now. There is this, Rat.
I set the traps. I laid the poison down.
What now? You hoped for matches, fire . . . burial?

Brett Mottram (15)
Ashby School, Ashby de la Zouch

I Am

I am nobody to many but somebody to me
I'm everything and yet nothing I can be
I'm lost yet I'm found, yet I'm lost once again
I hold in my power, my fears and my pain
I'm cold and I'm warm
Passionate and plain
I'm still learning about life
Though I've lived long enough
I'm petals of flowers and diamonds of rough
I crave a love that was never even there
I'm a whole of no pieces
A sum of no parts
I'm a pauper of aces
And a queen of hearts
I am who I am
With all ends and all starts.

Eloise Cundill (16)
Ashby School, Ashby de la Zouch

Memories Fade

The walls of my life are falling down on top of me.
The walls of my life are cracking, crumbling on top of me.
The love that fixed my walls together is fading,
fading in so many ways
and that is the reason why the binding of my walls
is disappearing, dissolving, disfigured.

I'm unimportant.
My reason is weakening and I have no security. No safety.
I have no one or nowhere to escape to.
There is no laughter, no playing, and no sense of light-heartedness to pin
my walls back up around me. And so they
fall,
fall,
fall on top of me.
There is no feeling. Just blank.
Just pain and hurt.

No love.
The love that held me up and made me strong,
and made me feel.
This love is just a distant memory, a memory of before.
And memories,
memories fade quickly.

Louise Simkin (16)
Ashby School, Ashby de la Zouch

So Sick

I'm so sick of you
And what you put me through
I was gonna leave all my luggage behind
Till I looked over my shoulder and saw your face
I'm glad I didn't change my mind
I'm so sick of fights
When we know I'm right
My heart's like an empty furnace or a broken clock
You gave me the fire I need, gave me the parts I lack
I don't want the memories of you, you can have them back
I'm so sick of your atmosphere
Why are you here?
Why am I so trusting?
Even my heart's started rusting
I'm so sick of falling for you
And the fact you want someone new
You said I have no heart, I have no soul and I have no brain
I tried to keep them alive but it was too much to sustain
I'm so sick of your power
Don't even feel safe in my tower
My safe-haven is invaded
My light has been shaded
The memories of you fade, but the scars on my heart remain
You're sat in my mind like what's left of a stain
I'm so sick of your influence over me
And the fact I'm too blind to see
That you will be
The death of me
The death of me
I'm so sick that you led me astray
I think it's time I stopped listening to you moan
It's like you're on freaking replay
I'm so sick of the fact that you make my day
God never answers me; I won't let it get me down
I just put my headphones in and turn up the sound
I'm so sick of you messing me around
I won't say goodbye
Maybe goodnight

I did this in spite
I'm so sick I wanna strangle you with the string of a kite
Burn out your eyes so you'll have no sight
And on this day
I will not be sick
I'll be brave
I'll be seen on the horizon
Dancing on your grave.

Callum Shaw (15)
Ashby School, Ashby de la Zouch

Tis I, Mistress Of Thee Mer

Yes.
'Tis I! 'Tis I!
Mistress of thee Mer
To wither and spindle through thy restless gather
Mine skin set alight as deep breath is consumed
For salutes my pleasure; sweet of thy tongue
Transfix the accent
Mine beating heart at which it skips - will start a tremor to turn a storm . . .

Fair hand clench to fist
Send magic to pulse
For all whispers sigh no more; dissolve as vapour in mine flesh
Water to thicken blood
Awaken to a new transition
To the soft labour breeze
Night falls upon!

Faith to defy air with force
A black with pearl robe, dance abyss
Waves of curls to match thy ocean
Eyes to shine a shimmer:

Topaz as the distant ocean floor
Sea-green jigsaw diamond shells
Cleanse blue - for it melts into me

Mine pupils reach eclipse.

Forwards mine voyager; for fight this elixir!
Draw me in to mirror a siren's call,
Orbit la lunar
She stands all alone
Send a silver pathway
Turn light to a sparkle

Hazed the surroundings
Absorb oneself to desire

For I am thee Mistress of thee Mer,
Summon me still
Turn to the day . . .

Amy Hodgkins (15)
Ashby School, Ashby de la Zouch

Over My Head - Stand No Longer

Hey you,
Why can't you stop this?
Why can't you stop the bitter anguish?
Putting everyone around
Down to depression
I still don't understand
You don't tell us anything
Already upset, you compose this worse

I'm supposed to love you
And what I'm supposed
Is truer than ever
But you can't help but bring me down
I find the news
I fall down further, you put me down
I don't know how to stand no longer

Maybe I should act my age
Maturity left behind me
I'm creeping up the stairs
A time beyond a seven-year-old
Keeping the silence
Like a game of Chinese whispers
In a dark dungeon at the edge of the Earth
It cannot end now, I'm hoping for later

I'm supposed to love you
And what I'm supposed
Is truer than ever
But you can't help but bring me down
I find the news
I fall down further, you put me down
I don't know how to stand no longer

This dark stress, as far as I view
The happiness came
And the happiness flew
It went just as fast
Left by a dank, dark, wet enemy
How am I supposed to keep myself up?
Advanced level of pain
It's all over my head

I'm supposed to love you
And what I'm supposed
Is truer than ever
But you can't help but bring me down
I find the news

I fall down further, you put me down
I don't know how to stand no longer
Over my head
Tell me how to stand
Over my head
Tell me how to stand
When I can no longer do this.

Ian Holland (16)
Ashby School, Ashby de la Zouch

I Write My Own Life - Mistakes

I write my own life,
Though 'tis a shame I write in pen,
The mistakes I cannot rub out,
The little mistakes I cannot change.

I write my own life,
My own goals that are never completed,
My wishes that never come true
And my dreams that are lost forever.

I write my own life,
The past, the present and the future,
Misunderstandings that went wrong,
Alterations that might come along.

I write my own life,
The world around me too,
I have good days and bad ones,
But so does everyone else.

I write my own life,
Though I am not alone,
People to help me correct myself,
To encourage me along the way.

I write my own life,
But this is where it ends,
Today I make a change
And tomorrow is a new beginning.

I write my own life,
Though 'tis a shame I write in pen,
The mistakes I cannot rub out,
But the mistakes I will never make again!

I write my own life,
Shame I write in pen . . .

Philippa Gibson (16)
Ashby School, Ashby de la Zouch

The Person

I'm surrounded by people
But I feel all alone
Things are said
Then things are done
But does anybody care?

At break time I sit
At lunchtime I stand
People try and talk to me
But I reply with a shrug
Does anybody care?

In lessons people whisper
Most likely about me
I sit and ignore it
It does no good
I'm a person, aren't I?

Who are my friends?
Who understands me?
Who ignores me on purpose?
Who am I?
I'm a person, aren't I?

Amelia Woodward (11)
Charlton School, Wellington

Red Is . . .

Red is . . . the colour of warm, dripping blood.
Red is . . . a flood of rage.
Red is . . . the colour of a lipstick kiss.
Red is . . . a poppy on a page.
Red . . . tastes like a juicy apple.
Red . . . smells like strawberries, nice and fresh.
Red . . . sounds like an evil cackle.
Red . . . feels like a long, silk dress.
Red . . . looks like sparkling rubies.
Red . . . makes me *stop!*
Red is . . . like sweet summer roses.
Red is . . . a bubblegum going *pop!*
Red is . . . the spaghetti Bolognese, I've been fed.
My favourite colour is . . . *red!*

Holly Phillips (12)
Charlton School, Wellington

Red!

Red is . . . the colour of blood
Red is . . . lips
Red is . . . rage
Red is . . . love
Red makes me . . . stop
Red looks like . . . shiny rubies
Red sounds like . . . an argument
Red smells like . . . summer roses
Red tastes like . . . juicy apples
Red is . . . *my favourite colour!*

Charlotte Price
Charlton School, Wellington

Pink

Pink is . . . the colour of a river dolphin.
Pink is . . . the perfect sunset.
Pink is . . . red and white mixed.
Pink is . . . a new crayon.
Pink smells like . . . sweets in a shop window.
Pink tastes like . . . the sweet taste of candyfloss.
Pink looks like . . . fairy cakes.
Pink feels like . . . a soft, cuddly teddy.
Pink makes me . . . think of strawberry milkshake.
Pink is my favourite colour!

Leia Jones (11)
Charlton School, Wellington

Chloe Howells

C hocolate melting in my mouth.
H appy people laughing.
L ovely lilies swaying in the breeze.
O ld people singing.
E ating picnics on the grass.

H ailstones falling.
O utside grey.
W ellington boots dripping.
E xcited children splashing.
L ittle babies crying.
L ong days inside.
S mall talk with nannies.

Chloe Howells (11)
Charlton School, Wellington

Blue

Blue is . . . the colour of the sky
Blue is . . . the ocean calm
Blue is . . . a burst of freedom
Blue is . . . a stream of calm
Blue tastes like . . . bubblegum
Blue looks like . . . dazzling sapphires
Blue feels like . . . the petals of a bluebell
Blue sounds like . . . the hum of a bluebottle
Blue makes me . . . think
Blue smells like . . . blueberry jam
Blue is my favourite colour.

Tyler Heayberd (12)
Charlton School, Wellington

Blue!

Blue is . . . the colour of paint
Blue is . . . a bad, sad colour
Blue is . . . a newborn sky
Blue looks like . . . sparkling aquamarine
Blue feels like . . . salty seawater
Blue sounds like . . . the turning of the tide
Blue smells like . . . a newborn bluebell
Blue makes me . . . shout to the world, 'Hi.'
Blue tastes like . . . a big batch of blueberries
Blue is the . . . colour of a cold
Blue is . . . my favourite colour.

Katie Meads (11)
Charlton School, Wellington

The Crocodile

Crocodile is . . . the red dark blood
Crocodile is . . . the orange staring eyes
Crocodile feels like . . . a chainmail of armour
Crocodile smells like . . . death and decay
Crocodile makes me . . . *weeeee!*
Crocodile is . . . my favourite friend.

Daniel McInnes (11)
Charlton School, Wellington

Charlton School

C oolest school in the world,
H igh it may be but it is still good,
A school full of corridors and stairs,
R acing tracks all around,
L ovely students and teachers,
T eachers are really cool,
O lder students helping younger ones,
N ew students getting lost in the maze of corridors and steps.

S eparate rooms for different subjects.
C harlton rocks and the teachers,
H igh scores and a better challenge,
O ther teachers helping out,
O h and we can't forget the school dinners, lovely,
L ost students finding their routes.

Amy Harley (12)
Charlton School, Wellington

Chocolate Spring

Chocolate
Rich, creamy, hard
Satisfying, milk, melted
Dark and white
Chocolate.

Roses
Red, curved
Perfumed, scented, bees
Summer, spring
Roses.

Lauren Armstrong (12)
Charlton School, Wellington

The Great Birds! - Haikus

Pigeons in the sky
Chirping, flying together
Fly, fly little birds

Eagles swooping down
Catching their prey for dinner
Birds flying away

Higher than ever
Pigeons are very lazy
But know other birds.

Thomas Camier
Charlton School, Wellington

I Dream For Fame

In my world, my dreams happen,
When night creeps in I become famous.
My head hits my cloud-like pillow,
As I sink into a deep, desiring dream.

My world is like Heaven,
I am a shimmering star in the night sky.
Being applauded by the atmosphere,
The black blanket of night softly whispers . . .

Fame and fortune in the sky of dreams,
Much more will come your way,
But beware things are not always what they seem,
For you will be forgotten at the break of day.

Then my heart pounds like a big base drum,
As the planets leave the sky.
The show is over, my fame has gone,
Until the night reaches me again.

But for now I must try hard,
To make my dreams reality.
I can always go back to my own world,
Where I am famous once again.

Dana Bott (12)
Charlton School, Wellington

The Other World

As I lay shivering cold,
Very young but looking old,
As drip-drops hit my head,
One day hopefully I will sleep in a bed.

As people pass by,
Nobody dares look me in my eye,
All I want is some coppers,
But nobody cares about 'dossers'.

As I lay in my sleeping bag,
I eat the last parts of my meal which makes me gag,
As my belly is churning,
My head is turning.

Thinking of my childhood a meal, a bed,
Back then life even wasn't that good, oooh I miss my ted,
It might be babyish but still a teddy is reassuring,
I wish it was morning.

I'm dying of hunger,
No food and my mind is like a bhangra,
Holes in my clothes,
So cold it's getting to my bones.

I'm telling you don't be homeless,
Just living in a house is good,
Any in fact, even if it's bad
You've still got warmth which is what I've never had.

Bradley Wood
Lancaster School for Boys, Leicester

It Is Autumn

It is autumn,
Bright leaves falling from the brittle trees above,
There is a dead silence,
You could hear a pin drop from a mile away.

The floor is oozing with colour just like a rainbow,
As it glistens.

Soon it is winter,
The world begins to change,
Snowmen appear, snow angels melt into the snowy floor,
Santa Claus comes out one night and gives you a big surprise.

Olly Rogers (12)
Newcastle-under-Lyme School, Newcastle-under-Lyme

My Winnie

I love my Winnie because she is as black as the dark night sky.
My cat peacefully purrs
Like the deep throaty tones of an Aston Martin.
Winnie loves dark, warm, steamy nights
So she can hunt for speedy, darting mice
As she sneaks back in with a deadly look in her eyes.
When the night is as black as Winnie
All you can see is the igniting green glow in her eyes.
When dawn breaks
She creeps in and finds a warm, cosy resting place.
My Winnie.

Tom Hatcher (12)
Newcastle-under-Lyme School, Newcastle-under-Lyme

My Dog

I love my dog like he loves his bone
Bouncing and bounding through the tall vibrant green grass
Leaping and licking, my little Luca
Walking him on hot sunny days
Makes me feel warm inside
His silky smooth brown coat glows in the sunset
Looking elegant as he trots along
He resembles the most beautiful animal
Although he loves his cuddles
He loves to play with his friends
And show his sinister grin
Over a bouncy ball between them all!

Megan Hughes (11)
Newcastle-under-Lyme School, Newcastle-under-Lyme

What Matters To Me?

They can be like the answer to boredom.
They can take time but don't seem that long.
They can be hilarious without trying.
They have lots of types for different people.
The sounds are deafening.
They are films.

Edward Ahearne (11)
Newcastle-under-Lyme School, Newcastle-under-Lyme

You Are

You're not perfect.
Nobody is,
but you don't try to be
and that's what I love.

You're not afraid
to be different,
to stand out in a crowd,
like a rose among thorns.

You're not a little child anymore
but you kick the autumn leaves,
waving your arms,
reaching for the sun.

You're not a hero.
You've done nothing special.
Nobody knows your name
but to me . . .

You're everything.

Lydia Carr (14)
Newcastle-under-Lyme School, Newcastle-under-Lyme

What Matters Most

I do care not for fame.
The thought of a crowd fighting to catch a glimpse unnerves me.
This house does not dabble in politics nor finance.
Intellect, the concept of pleonastically perplexing a person's parietal lobe
not that it matters.

I care for what I can do for people;
an impact for the greater good of people.
A lasting legacy for people to be thankful for,
whether in the arts, sciences or diplomacy.

I could be a great painter or writer . . . or both.
Releasing creative thoughts loose onto a blank canvas
not hanging on the walls of galleries,
but in the homes of the world.
For onlookers to be proud of.

A scientist optimising the world,
adjusting switches, valves and consorting with leading academics.
I'd experiment in psychology.
Why do people want to stop others fulfilling their dreams?
In a hope of people finally being united together.

If that is the case, I'd be a diplomat,
not analysing these problems but fixing them.
Bringing two sides together;
not to enforce their beliefs, but, to reach a middle path.

I might not succeed in changing humanity
I do not care if I don't.
I care for doing,
no matter the outcome,

knowing that I've tried.
For if you can see, look
and if you can look, observe
once observed next to act.
To make an impact.
That is what I care for.

Philip Eccleston (14)
Newcastle-under-Lyme School, Newcastle-under-Lyme

Home Sweet Home

I land at Manchester Airport,
I rush through passport control,
I hurry into a heated taxi
And make my journey home.

I push my way through the door,
I stop,
I see my home,
Warmth fills me inside
And I collapse on the sofa.

I slowly and quietly unlock the door to my bedroom,
I feel like it's the first time I've seen it,
Photos of my friends and family crowd my desk,
Familiar faces make me smile,
I relax on my beanbag,
Too tired to unpack . . .

The smell of fish and chips,
Creeps down the hallway,
It reaches my room
And wavers temptingly in front of my nose,
I sprint down the hallway,
Where my family are sitting at the table.

I curl up on the sofa,
Next to my dog
And watch the TV,
In front of a log burning fire.

No words can describe the feeling of home,
Apart from it's the best feeling of all.

Abbie Keats (14)
Newcastle-under-Lyme School, Newcastle-under-Lyme

What Matters To Me

My grandma often declares
'The best things in life are free.'
Yeah, I think, flippantly
That's really trite
But, deep down, I know she's right

What matters are people, family and friends
Love that never ends
People, places, loved ones' faces
That kind of thing

However, at this moment in my life
I'm at that awkward age
Self-obsessed and full of rage
And it's not that I disagree
It's just that I can't help being me

I'm into superficial stuff
In fact I cannot get enough
Youtube, music, films, reality TV,
These are the things that matter to me

Other things really matter
Like my nightly Facebook chatter
Talking without lips
Exchanging sarcastic quips

Amongst the things I highly rate
Is staying up really late
Drinking unhealthy drinks
And eating fast food without a plate

I love to play on my PS3
Excitement in virtual reality
Killing, racing, vicariously
Moronic games are what matter to me!

Call me shallow, call me mad
Superficial, hollow, sad
Just a stupid teenage lad
However, world peace would make me glad

What matters are people, family and friends
Love that never ends
People, places, loved ones' faces
That kind of thing.

Peter Przyslo (14)
Newcastle-under-Lyme School, Newcastle-under-Lyme

Life

What lies beyond this mystic realm?
What dark beings lurk between my twisted thoughts?
The four walls of this room begin to close.
Every day the same,
There is no escape
From this nightmare.

I feel trapped
In pain and
Lost within myself.

What do I want?
What do I hope for?
What can I expect?

Richard Garner (14)
Newcastle-under-Lyme School, Newcastle-under-Lyme

Whispa - My Cat

Whispa rubs persistently against my legs.
I pat her methodically.
Her tiny motor inside
Purrs intensely -
A gentle, little whirr.

I chatter to her, whispering.
She licks me back, softly:
Though she can't talk
And I can't purr,
We understand each other
As siblings would.
I am human
But Whispa — a cat.

Samina Bana (14)
Newcastle-under-Lyme School, Newcastle-under-Lyme

Flora

Every day.
Waking up
To the little chirrups in the morning,
To soften the blow of a 7 o'clock start.
Her soft black nose buried asleep within the hay
Snuffling around looking to play.

When her food is given,
The accidental nibbling on the tips of my fingers
Never fails to make me smile.
And after school,
The excitement
Of her playing hide-and-seek
And looking for something to eat.

And the pungent smell
Of her soft, black fur.
Her beautiful, black eyes,
The window to her soul,
Give me hope on the darkest of days.
Filling me with joy
And guiding me on,
Making her my little ray of sun.

Oh how I cherish my guinea pig,
Words cannot do her justice
And demonstrate my love for her,
I will always love her delicate purr.

Natasha Brian (14)
Newcastle-under-Lyme School, Newcastle-under-Lyme

Xavier

His influence, above all others
is what matters.
What he says, when he says it.
It may be derogatory,
in fact it probably is
but that doesn't matter.
He's here.
That matters.

His noise,
his music,
his presence, so perfectly presented.
I still hear and feel him,
through what he left behind.
An empty room, full of noise.
An empty shelf, full of music.
An empty room.
Filled by Xavier.

Arnaud Lacey (14)
Newcastle-under-Lyme School, Newcastle-under-Lyme

Tommy

I love Tommy like a tree loves its leaves,
He's silent and shouting and smiley and soft.
He's loud but invisible just like a cold windy day.
You might wonder who he is but only I know.
He's white or blue or yellow or green.
He's exclusive and private and dazzling to me.
He dashes to dodge you when you ponder around.
Do you know who he is?
He's Tommy, my invisible friend!

Jemma Richards (11)
Newcastle-under-Lyme School, Newcastle-under-Lyme

Home Is Where The Heart Is

Close to me yet far away,
She watches over day
                    By
                          Day.
Not tangible but her presence is felt;
When memories sinking resurface . . .

Never seen but always there;
To listen or simple to care.
Taken away, it wasn't time
A lesson learnt and
                          Values
                                Change.

Feels like my heart will never mend . . .
It gets easier as time goes on.
But I can't replace what is gone . . .

So to answer what is important to me,
Is memories and family.
Not in places far away,
Nor in materialistic trinkets;
But in my house, behind
                          My
                                Gate
Lies a welcoming safe haven.

Home is where my heart is.

Catherine Hibbert (15)
Newcastle-under-Lyme School, Newcastle-under-Lyme

What Matters To Me?

What you mean to me
Is everything in the world.
You're the one who understands me
And you were my shoulder to cry on.
Throughout our journey together,
You've stuck with me
Through thick
And thin times.

I love everything about you;
Your laughter and happiness
Put a smile on my face.
I've had some really good times with you.
When we argue,
I want you to know
That I still care about you.
You will never know
That I'm writing about you
Simply because you don't know
The big role you play in my life:
You are simply the best.

Kar Lai Fong (14)
Newcastle-under-Lyme School, Newcastle-under-Lyme

My Kittens

My kittens mean the world to me
With their playful games and excitement,
How they make me feel warm inside.
They remind me of a gorgeous sunny day,
With an oozing cool breeze.
My kittens make me happy when I'm sad.
They turn my frown upside down.
I love my kittens so much.

Cameron Anderson (11)
Newcastle-under-Lyme School, Newcastle-under-Lyme

What Matters To Me

Harry Potter matters to me,
Many a night I will stay up to read them.
The seventh is my favourite.
Its name being 'Harry Potter and the Deathly Hallows'.
I like it for many reasons.
It is full of magic and mystery.
A war and love.

My fish matters to me.
His name is Beavis.
He is a koi carp.
He is orange, black and yellow.
He is older than me.
He is 40cm.
He lives in a pond.
I love him.

My life matters to me,
Matters a lot more than my possessions,
Matters as though the world would end without it.
That seems impossible but it's true.
Because when my life ends
The whole world will end
But, only from my point of view.

Leah Edmends (11)
Newcastle-under-Lyme School, Newcastle-under-Lyme

My Family

Families wouldn't be families without arguments,
Families wouldn't be families without laughs,
So when I think about my sister, mum and dad
And all the really good times that we've had,
I think it's fair to say,
Although we've had our moments of dismay
That we're a normal, loving family.

James Birchall (11)
Newcastle-under-Lyme School, Newcastle-under-Lyme

What Matters To Me

Catching, kicking the ball,
Making a run,
Tackling as hard as I can.
Scoring a try,
Goal!
Winning the match
Is what matters to me.

My friend
Always there for me
When I get hurt,
Letting me borrow his things.
So polite
And that is what matters to me.

The sizzling pizza in the oven,
The tomatoes exploding in my mouth,
Chocolate melting in the microwave
That's what matters to me.

Beinn Yule (11)
Newcastle-under-Lyme School, Newcastle-under-Lyme

What Matters To Me

Weekends are my favourite times.
My dad comes home from work.
Saturdays are swallowed up by sport.
First there is squash and then there's ballet.
Often I visit my nana and we go to the farmers' market.

Sundays are the busiest time.
Mum and Dad are always doing jobs
Throughout the summer.
My biggest job is picking the raspberries;
My favourite fruit.

The best family time is Sunday evening.
Nana comes and
We all have a big roast dinner.
Then, all too soon, it is Monday again.

Emilia Wyatt (11)
Newcastle-under-Lyme School, Newcastle-under-Lyme

Rugby

I love rugby
The adrenalin rush
The players on the pitch
The whistle goes
Everybody roaring and waiting for the scoring
The crowd want more
The stadium is alive, the singing when a team score
The game ends with a great score
The fans are pleased but want more!

Simon Mitchell (12)
Newcastle-under-Lyme School, Newcastle-under-Lyme

What Matters To Me

There I was lying excitedly in my bed,
Warm and cosy, staring out of the window,
Watching the snowflakes perform their dance,
Flickering in the night sky.
Christmas!
My eyes were simply refusing to shut . . .
I just couldn't wait!
I could feel my heart dancing,
Like fireworks with the delicate snowflakes.
I concentrated . . .
There was a sort of jingle bell noise ringing outside,
As if it was on the roof.
Why?
What was the noise . . . ?
Santa!
I shut my eyes,
Hoping he wouldn't enter my room.
A ray of light shone through my bedroom.
I began counting my sheep, one sheep, two sheep, three sheep, four sh . . .

Gregory Garner (12)
Newcastle-under-Lyme School, Newcastle-under-Lyme

Millie

The startling white patches that once circled her eyes,
Now turning a faint grey colour.
Her jet-black body, still the same but now fully grown.
Once she was able to move so gracefully yet energetically at the same time,
Now her run is laboured and her pace that of a snail.
Her deep brown eyes with a playful glint in the corner,
The only thing that remains identical, reminding me she's still the little puppy
she was so long ago,
No matter how much her body is telling me otherwise.

Holly Woodward (12)
Newcastle-under-Lyme School, Newcastle-under-Lyme

What Matters To Me

What matters to me?
What matters to me is . . .
Standing on the top of the ski slope ready to race down,
Persuading Mummy to let me have a mobile phone,
Cycling to Llandudno before I was eleven,
Climbing Ben Nevis when I was nine
And also, my family and friends matter to me.

But what matters most to me
Is *Mummy!*

I always feel so happy and comforted when I am near her.
I love her and she is always there for me.
She looks after me, encourages me and believes in me.

That's why Mummy matters to me the most!

Abigail Binnington (11)
Newcastle-under-Lyme School, Newcastle-under-Lyme

My Sister

Her brown eyes twinkle as bright as stars
Her black hair luscious and soft
Her fair skin soft to touch
Lashes long and curled above big round eyes
As vibrant as the colours of trees in autumn
As beautiful as a jewel
My best friend
Sensitive yet tough
Clever and pretty
Smart and witty.

Arya Ghatge (11)
Newcastle-under-Lyme School, Newcastle-under-Lyme

What Matters To Me

My family matters to me
But the person who matters
Most is my mum.

My cousin, Harrison,
Matters to me because
He makes me laugh and always
Feel happy when I'm down.

My swimming matters to me
Like it does to Michael Phelps,
Because knowing when
I've won makes me feel as though I've
Just accomplished the best thing ever.

My cat also matters to me
Because I love it when she
Cuddles up to me and starts to purr.

All these things matter to me
Because they're all the things I love.

Eleanor Pomiankowski (12)
Newcastle-under-Lyme School, Newcastle-under-Lyme

What Matters To Me

A lot of things matter to me.
Some of them are big and some are small.
Freddie, my dog, matters to me
And so does the rest of my family.
He has soft fur.
Nearly as soft as silk.
He's very greedy!
Sometimes when I sit down for tea I find there is none left
Because it's in his tummy!
The same thing happens with my dad
And a packet of chocolate digestive biscuits . . .
One second there will be a full packet
And the next they will have magically disappeared!
Of course my mum and dad mean a lot to me
And the rest of my family.
My mum also means a lot to me
And I wish you could try her chicken curry.
It's as hot as fire!
My friends are also special to me,
Including Ellie, Maia and Bethany.
My grades also matter to me.
My face lights up like a light bulb when I get As!
As you can see, a lot of things matter to me!

Olivia Rhodes (11)
Newcastle-under-Lyme School, Newcastle-under-Lyme

Chocolate!

In the forbidden cupboard,
above the cooker,
is where the treasure lies.
A milky heaven,
a melting perfection,
all wrapped up in tinfoil coats.

Smooth and creamy in your mouth,
gliding over taste buds,
the taste of cocoa beans fills your senses,
the delicious happiness as you swallow,
chocolate.

Emma Shepherd (12)
Newcastle-under-Lyme School, Newcastle-under-Lyme

What Matters To Me

Cats, because I have two.
Dogs, because I love them.
Family, because I can trust them.
Friends, because they're mine.
But most of all horses.
Those magical creatures
So elegant and smooth,
So fast and sleek.

I know my family is important.
My friends are great to me
But really,
I love horses best.
I love it when I get chocolate.
It's great when I get lasagne,
But when I ride my horse,
It's better than all the rest.

Elizabeth Chapman (11)
Newcastle-under-Lyme School, Newcastle-under-Lyme

My Cat, Warwick

My cat, Warwick, is as dopey as a doughnut,
He's a silly, stupid, short-tempered fluffball
And he crashes around my house
Like a headless chicken.
Thinking about Warwick makes my tummy
Feel gooey with laughter.
My cat is a bright, yellow, warm, sunny day,
Where everything happens to go wrong.
Warwick has an interesting character
And has some rather strange tricks up his sleeve,
But he's still my cat,
Warwick.

Alice Lovett (11)
Newcastle-under-Lyme School, Newcastle-under-Lyme

The Netball Morning

As we walk onto the court,
We see the other team walk on court,
At about 9am in the morning,
The sun glistening,
Then the coin is tossed,
We win the toss,
As the centre gets ready to pass,
Whistle is blown,
Run and catch if you can,
Get it into the circle and shoot,
We score,
1-0!

Charlotte Thorley (12)
Newcastle-under-Lyme School, Newcastle-under-Lyme

My Friends

My friends matter to me
As God matters to Christians,
My friends,
They are amazing,
Academic,
Outstanding,
All at the same time!
Being with my friends is like
The sunniest day in the world,
Really bright
And shining.
My friends are to me
Like a yellowy orange,
Always warm and a radiant light in my life.
We get along like cream and butter,
A smooth paste forming a cake mixture.
We are
Always
There for each other.

Alice Corfield (11)
Newcastle-under-Lyme School, Newcastle-under-Lyme

Chocolate

I love chocolate,
As much as I love shoes.
Crisp
Chunky chocolate,
Melting in my mouth,
Then *crunch.*
After a victorious win in netball,
A Galaxy does the trick.
Hot chocolate is a good one,
For a snowy winter's night.
The chocolate,
Brown as an old leather boot,
Trickles down my throat.
The sugar,
The calories,
Who cares when it comes to chocolate?
Only a treat,
Only one,
Only a present,
It's only chocolate.

Sophia Panayi (11)
Newcastle-under-Lyme School, Newcastle-under-Lyme

Darcy!

Her tiny grey woolly face looks at me
With her great big hazelnut eyes begging for a bite of my food
She shoos away the cats, just in case
Barking right down their ears
My dog, Darcy, is one of the cats' worst fears
She runs around the garden madly
Stalking through the mud
Barking at any squeak she hears
But that's why I love her
My dog, Darcy!

Izzie Davenport (12)
Newcastle-under-Lyme School, Newcastle-under-Lyme

My Wonderful Family

I love my family because they make me laugh
They show love and affection towards me and each other.
They are explosions, everyone never stops interesting me,
Grandad telling stories of war and destruction
Showing me gadgets he kept.
They are like sunbeams, brilliant
They are rainbows in the deep blue cloudless sky.
They are graceful horses, elegant and beautifully excellent,
My family, they are great,
My family, they are magnificent.

James Smith (11)
Newcastle-under-Lyme School, Newcastle-under-Lyme

What Matters To Me?

What matters to me?
Books.
Magic, murder, adventure, suspicion, funny, mysterious,
old or modern. They open up worlds to enjoy and imagine, to have fun and -
a good read.

What matters to me?
Food.
Delicious, scrumptious, gorgeous, mouth-watering,
stomach-satisfying, crumbling, soft, hard, sour, sweet - *mmmmmmm* . . .
food. The aftertaste of chocolate in my mouth, the warmth of a freshly baked
cake.

What matters to me?
Sports.
The thrill of the tackle as the mud splats in my face, the
enjoyment of the twang as the tennis ball hits the racket,
the marvel of how far and fast the cricket ball goes as my
bat swings . . . the adrenaline-pumping feeling of sports.

What matters to me?
Family.
The warm embrace of a hug, snuggling under a blanket
watching TV, sitting down together eating tea, having
great times with my family.

And that's what matters to me.

Daniel Badger (12)
Newcastle-under-Lyme School, Newcastle-under-Lyme

What Matters To Me

What matters to me
most is my family's life.
That's my greatest thought.

What matters to me,
also is education.
It helps us in life.

What matters to me,
is global warming. We should
stop it getting worse.

What matters to me,
is my pet's health and safety.
It's my place to care.

What matters to me,
is what I'm going to be when
I become a man.

James Edward John McKinnon (11)
Newcastle-under-Lyme School, Newcastle-under-Lyme

Chocolate

I love chocolate.
The melt in your mouth feeling,
and creamy flavour.
Smooth and milky,
delicately carved into a beautiful shape.
A tough decision,
Galaxy or Cadbury?
A guilty pleasure,
when no one's there!
Melt it with strawberries or marshmallows.
The ruby-red fruit,
with the snow-white chocolate.
I love chocolate.

Rob Beckett (12)
Newcastle-under-Lyme School, Newcastle-under-Lyme

Sledging

On a cold, dark, snowy day
Flying down a hill
Seems like a good idea
The sub-zero temperatures try to stop me
But I never give in
As I go down the hill

Sledging can be scary
Sometimes fast, sometimes slow
But always fun
As the bracing wind
Hits you straight in the face
As I fly down the hill
On a cold snowy day.

David Trillo (13)
Newcastle-under-Lyme School, Newcastle-under-Lyme

The Charity Shop

The charity shop dressed up like an Aladdin's cave
With bright vibrant colours waiting to be seen.
You'll never know what you may find
Ruffling through those great designs.
Every single thing's like a piece of treasure
Waiting to be turned into gold.
That lovely patterned dress,
Those purple metallic shoes,
That necklace you could wear with that new dress.
You're guaranteed to find something that will catch your eye
As you get out your old tatty purse to pay for your purchases
Something catches your eye,
That lonely animal print purse you could buy.
It's much better than the one you have
So you buy it
Well you may as well!

India Mellor (11)
Newcastle-under-Lyme School, Newcastle-under-Lyme

What Matters To Me?

The leaves swirled down.
They crunched underfoot.
The sun shone, but it was nippy.
I was warm,
Wrapped up in scarf and gloves.
Bliss.

The snow flitted down.
The sun was near,
Yet so cold.
I was, again, warm.
Bliss.

The lambs spring about.
The blossom flew down.
Dressed in T-shirt and shorts,
I was cool.
Bliss . . .
The kids lazed on the beach,
The waves flirted up.
Everyone in swimming costumes.
I was cool.

Katy Polles (13)
Newcastle-under-Lyme School, Newcastle-under-Lyme

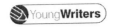

The Cycle Race

I love that sound,
A full carbon disc wheel zooming past,
It's like an aeroplane taking off a runway,
Thousands standing and cheering,
They come through the line,
The crowd lifts as the big brass bell rings continuously,
The chase is on,
The S-Ram cranks grind round, the bike swaying from one side to the other,
As the crowd steps up,
The pace steps up, the race steps up,
Ten kilometres to go, fifteen minutes,
The white jerseys of HTC line up at the front,
Mark Cavendish at the back,
Five minutes to go, four kilometres,
Two riders left, Cavendish and Renshaw,
Hushovd comes up, speeding alongside,
'Where is the man from the Isle of Man?' says the commentator,
Then Cavendish bullets past in front of the camera and wins,
The race is over.

Ben Meir (12)
Newcastle-under-Lyme School, Newcastle-under-Lyme

The Garden

The garden is a wonderful place,
With lush green grass
And the beautiful blossoming flowers.
The gorgeous smell of freshly cut grass.
The lovely sound of the birds,
As they sit in the trees.
The bees fly around the garden,
Busy collecting pollen.

This, however, is in the summer.
Over the year it gradually changes,
The leaves go orange and brown.
The flowers begin to die down
And eventually all the leaves fall off the trees.
During the winter the garden looks like a blank canvas,
Waiting for the artist to paint it spring.

Tom Cowling (12)
Newcastle-under-Lyme School, Newcastle-under-Lyme

The Kingfisher

I squat down carefully,
In my dull camouflaged suit,
Waiting for that lightning blue flash,
To appear in my tired eyes,
The giant red stag calling in the hazy background,
His voice filling the cold air with warmth,
Suddenly the fluffy chicks start to call vigorously,
I await the sight of the magnificent bird,
I look through my huge camera lens steadily,
Even that,
I have covered with camouflaged equipment,
Then,
I see it,
That beautiful blue streak,
The wings beat rapidly under the morning light,
It picks up a small silver fish,
From the shiny, shimmering, flowing river
And then rushes into his nest,
As if he spotted me in the hidden hide,
As soon as he left,
I never saw him for another agonising hour,
Then,
Suddenly,
I see him flying behind me,
I didn't want to move in case I disturbed him,
But,
I don't have to,
He comes to me,
Cautiously,
He lands on a perfectly placed stick,
With the dazzling sun on it,
Shining brightly,

Now right in front of me,
A perfect shot of a kingfisher,
I press the shutter,
Now on my camera the most amazing picture of a kingfisher,
I crept out the hide absolutely flabbergasted.

Tim Bramall (12)
Newcastle-under-Lyme School, Newcastle-under-Lyme

Unique

I am unique and so is the world,
It makes me wonder who I will be
And what I am about to see,
So what makes me so special?
But it is fun being me.

Being unique is a great gift,
It doesn't matter if I am weird or not,
People say that they are jealous of what talents I've got,
It feels so unusual,
But it is fun being me.

Sometimes people try and copy me,
Because of who I am,
It makes me happy that someone thinks I can,
I like my friends the way they are,
Whether they are incredibly brilliant,
Or unbelievably strange,
But it is fun being me.

I try to be normal,
Or be me,
It is a challenge like the spelling bee,
It is a struggle,
But there is a way,
Deep down in my red hot flaming heart,
But it is really fun being me.

I feel so alive,
It feels so pure,
Being unique,
But most of all . . .
It is fun being me!

Freya Umataliev (12)
Newport Girls' High School, Newport

A Poem - Or Maybe Not

What makes a poem a poem?
And why isn't it a story?
Does it have some kind of quality,
Like lines that end in rhyme?

Or does it have a rhythm,
A captivating beat,
That makes it sound more interesting,
But can't have too many syllables in one line or it doesn't sound right?

Now I think I know what poems are,
I'm glad I've got this clear.
Now please do me the favour of answering this terribly confusing question;
Is this a story or a poem?

Ali Scott (14)
Newport Girls' High School, Newport

Home

(This is how I felt when my autistic brother, Harvey, ran away . . . Luckily we did find him afterwards, but at the time I was devastated. It was very scary!)

Home is where the heart is?
Where is your heart taking you?
Is there something we need to do?
It's hard to imagine, where you want to be,
Where you will enjoy yourself, like you used to with me,
How can we make it better, it's been hard for both of us,
For you to go away as quickly as the morning gust.

Home is where the heart is?
I just want you to know
That we will do anything for you to come back home.

Emily Chapman (12)
Newport Girls' High School, Newport

Train Of Thought

I sat there with my notebook,
Listening to the birds tweet
When suddenly I heard a whistle
So very soft and sweet.

Lurking in the shadows,
Yet staying so very clear
I heard the clickety-clack of the wheels
As the train began to draw near.

I flipped the pages over
But not a rustling sound was heard;
A chugging noise was produced
As the train carried on undeterred.

Noisily and vividly,
The train began to appear
Yet the birds around me stayed:
They did not fly away in fear.

Suddenly the train arrived,
Smoke engulfed my lungs and face.
There on the page was my poem
And silence fell over the place.

Lucy Simmonds (13)
Newport Girls' High School, Newport

The Sunrise

This morning I saw the birth of the sun,
Like it is new to this world.
The reddy-orange sky at the height of its beauty,
The beginning for some, the end for others.

The tip of the fiery, red sun emerges,
Like it came from underground.
Slowly, it rises marking the start of the day,
The birds start to tweet and sing.

The dewdrops on the grass,
Like diamonds in a rock.
Shimmering in the light of the arising sun,
Behind it is the key to the season ahead.

The sun starts to appear as a semi-circle,
The dark blue of the night begins to fade.
The light begins to seep through,
Strengthening the blue of the morning sky.

The sun climbs higher in the sky,
Warming the air as it rises.
The life around it is clearly seen,
A new day has been born.

Beth Evans (13)
Newport Girls' High School, Newport

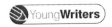

The Hedgehog

'You may begin,' rings the voice,
A hundred papers flip.
My eyes scan the page,
Heart thumping; it is too hot.

The words make no sense,
They spiral round my head.
Weaving and tumbling,
It is getting hotter still.

All around me, pens move,
Scurrying across pages.
Minds are working.
Mine is not.

Through my mind's eye
I see nothing.
Only darkness.
A threatening blankness.

Panic engulfs me,
Time is running out.
I try to stay calm
And an image forms.

A hedgehog rustles leaves,
Snuffling and squeaking.
It shrinks back when I move closer.
An idea still eludes me.

The hedgehog curls itself into
A spiky ball; I cannot touch it.
I can write nothing,
An idea still evades me.

Till I reach over two fingers
And tickle its neck.
It uncurls, relaxes
And stares with deep brown eyes.

Ideas suddenly wash over me,
Inspiration floods my mind.
My tension eases as, one-by-one,
The pages are written.

Alex Gormley (13)
Newport Girls' High School, Newport

Mixed Up Fairy Stories

Once upon a time there lived
Three bears
Who hated Cinderella
Because of her warty complexion.

Goldilocks broke into their house
And chopped off Rapunzel's hair
And ate all of their
Three blind mice.

The prince charged up to
The gingerbread house
And destroyed the
Fairy Godmother.

Then Tom Thumb
Rode a broom
And had a woodcutter bring back
A gingerbread man.

The seven dwarves
Ate a marzipan heart
Who laughed at the ugly sisters
When their house fell down.

The three pigs ran
To the evil witch
And locked her away in a tower
With a magic mirror.

The mirror told the Queen
That her porridge had been eaten.
She flew into a rage and fell through the floor
And fell asleep for a hundred years.

The prince's kiss woke her up
And he ran away
Because he had to
Pull the sword from the stone.

He left some breadcrumbs
Which danced away with the Pied Piper
And flew off to Neverland
To go to a ball with Cinderella.

Cinderella cried,
The three bears died
And the pigs flew over the moon
And they all lived happily ever after!

Natasha Bodger (13)
Newport Girls' High School, Newport

The Flower Of Thought

A falling seed lands upon the ground,
Its burial was soon to come,
Its soul rested upon the floor,
But its life had just begun.

It started to grow
And to twist and to turn
As raindrops fell to the floor
The leaves moved and opened.

As the plant began to shake and swirl
A flower bud was produced.
Its journey had been long and bright
But its colour had now faded.

The bud was finally opened,
The petals then spread out,
The colours were so vivid and bright
And the sun gave nutrients to it.

But as quick as its journey had begun,
The flower started to quiver,
For the flower had no time left here,
So it began to close and shrivel.

Just as the sun began to rise,
The poem page was printed,
A flower so bold and so unique
Had now settled on the earth.

Bethany Slater (13)
Newport Girls' High School, Newport

Autumn's Here

Autumn's here
It's that time of year
When the leaves change colour to red, gold and brown
The big, shiny conkers are falling to the ground, down and down
The nights are turning chilly
As I peer out of the window the squirrel is acting rather silly
The fire burns bright
On this cold dark night
Autumn's here
It's that time of year.

Ciara Hogan (11)
Newport Girls' High School, Newport

Home Is . . .

Home is where you go when you need a friend
Home is where you go when you are sad and lonely
Home is where you go when you need help
Home is where you go to be loved and cared for

Home is a place you go when you are scared
Home is a place you want when you are lost
Home is a place to hide when you need quiet
Home is a place to find a shoulder to cry on

A home is something that you need to make a family complete
A home is something that is not just bricks and mortar
A home is something which is secure when locked up safe
A home is something always full of laughter and love

You need a home to help you feel complete
You need a home to help keep a family safe
You need a home to contain a family's happiness
You need a home to come home to each night.

Olivia Johnson (11)
Newport Girls' High School, Newport

The Old Man

He sits in his chair,
Smiling and dreaming
Of a world that he once knew
But now it is gone,
He tries to move on
As what else can a man do?

He dreams of a place
Where the mockingbird sings
And where flowers smile up to the sun.
He runs and he plays
As every child does,
The happy, intelligent one.

But the noise of the world
Brings him awake
And his childhood gets left far behind.
His dreaming is done
Of that place in the sun
In his tired, wizened, old mind.

Jessica Llewellyn (13)
Newport Girls' High School, Newport

Home

I see myself - with my friends skipping down the street to my house.
As if it was only yesterday . . .
I see myself creeping up to my brothers' bedroom door, quiet as a mouse.
As if it was only yesterday . . .
I see myself in the sweet shop smelling the sweet smell of chocolate and
honeycomb.
As if it was only yesterday . . .
I see myself smelling the sweet smell of home.
I fall out of bed - *bang* as I hit the floor,
This unfamiliar house is mocking me once again.

Megan Jones (12)
Newport Girls' High School, Newport

There Is No Place Like Home!

My home is so big, so comforting,
My home is a place where I am safe,
My home is a place I can be me,
My home is a part of me,
There is no place like home!

In my kitchen,
Inviting smells of home-made spaghetti,
Kettle boiling, steam spiralling,
Cupboards full of mouth-watering food,
There is no place like home!

In my lounge,
Fire crackling, heating the room,
Music tinkling from the piano,
Family crowded around the big TV,
There is no place like home!

In my bathroom,
A big hot bath full of bubbles,
Lotions and potions line the shelves,
Condensation on the windows,
There is no place like home!

In my room,
My comfy, warm bed so soft and snuggly,
A desk where I work, piled high with books,
My wardrobe full of dazzling new clothes,
There is no place like home!

My home is big, so comforting,
My home is a place where I am safe,
My home is a place I can be me,
My home is a part of me,
There is no place like home!

Caitlin Webb (11)
Newport Girls' High School, Newport

A Stable Home

My house has a door but no windows,
The walls are painted with big rosettes and bows.

I lie on a bed with straw and hay,
You can forget the expense of a duvet.

Is that the rattle of the gate I hear?
The crunching of wellies makes me cheer.

Here comes my breakfast for today,
Will it be bacon, muesli or just chopped hay?

I'm not interested in mashed potato, the peelings are fine,
All that vitamin C makes me shine.

Oh no! What's that?
Oh help! It's that dreaded tack!

I walk to the field as fast as a tiger,
I really don't think exercise is worth all this mither!

My hooves are picked out now,
It's like she's digging for gold.

The soothing strokes of the brush,
Makes me very sleepy, hushhh, hushhh.

My slumber doesn't last as she moves to my tail,
Oh dear! It's tangled again, that comb doesn't half make me wail!

Oh the joys, I'm back in my field,
Now my mind is relaxed and healed.

Did you guess? I'm a horse! Of course!

Alice Bratton (11)
Newport Girls' High School, Newport

My Pencil Case

My pencil case is full of things that I need for school,
If you forget your pencil case then you are quite a fool,
It has all the things you need for a typical school day,
If you forget your pencil case then you will have to pay.

My compass twirls as it makes a perfect circle,
My protractor I love as it is purple,
My calculator loves to sit and do some division
And my pink pen likes to help me with some revision.

My favourite blue pen is a wonder as it seems,
The beautiful blue colour twinkles and gleams,
Then there is my black pen, cool and strong and tough,
Not even my hand can do as much as leave a smudge!

All of my pencil crayons love to come and play
And if something is white they'll colour it straight away,
They love to make things presentable, they'd never let me scribble,
They won't even let me lose a little dribble!

My rubber is a neat freak, he hates to see a mess,
So don't worry if making a mistake, he'll clean it up, don't stress,
My ruler hates to see a squiggly line,
He likes it to be straight, he does it in no time!

There are many reasons that I love my pencil case,
If someone ever stole it I would start a great big chase!
So never go and lose it,
Or I'll hit you - just a little bit.

Ellie Jones (11)
Newport Girls' High School, Newport

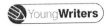

Poem

Have you ever written a poem?
It's really, really hard.
I don't know where to begin,
So I'll start right at the start.

What shall my theme be?
Snowflakes? Dragons? Dreams?
I'll start out writing nothing
And it'll turn into reams and reams.

I'm getting on quite well now.
I'm already on verse three.
Now, what rhymes with three then?
Three, free, pea, me!

I'll say something about myself.
I'm weird, but wonderful too.
I have lots of funny friends,
They laugh when I type 'poo'.

I'm stuck for ideas again,
I'm a bit of a fool.
You may think it's a boring topic,
But I'll write about my school.

I go to Newport Girls,
With all of my bestest friends.
We are the coolest of the lot,
We set all the trends!

Not really, we're a group of freaks,
We're always mucking about.
We're quite bad in class sometimes,
We laugh and joke and shout.

I'm at the end of the page right now.
I'll have to say goodbye.
I hope you liked my poem.
I hope you didn't cry.

So now you've read the whole shebang!
The snap, the crackle, the pop.
This is getting all too random.
I think I'm going to *stop!*

Pagan Hunt (12)
Newport Girls' High School, Newport

My Fantasy World

Surrounded by my fantasy world;
Silent and unknown
Soft, cool breeze touches my face like silk sheets on a bed.

Palm trees wave, beckoning,
Golden sand, slips between my toes,
Above a clear blue sky,
Gazes down on this paradise.

Lush vegetation, tropical wonderland,
Splashes of vibrant colour surround,
I drink in the deep scent of flowers
And dizzy, I stumble aground.

The dark, intoxicated hand of night,
Creeps over the tranquil, turquoise sea,
Turning the inky depths to midnight-blue,
As conversations still within my world and me.

Hermione Baulf (12)
Newport Girls' High School, Newport

I Live On Planet Zog!

I live on Planet Zog
Where everything's upside down
It is full of chocolate bogs
And everything spins around

I live on Planet Zog
Where everyone is so happy
The best drink is eggnog
We can't eat anything solid (our teeth are gappy)

I live on Planet Zog
Where it snows custard all year round
We love to go for a jog
And we live in a dirt mound

I live on Planet Zog!

Natasha Lewis (11)
Newport Girls' High School, Newport

Hunting?

Stalking, stalking
The tall grass barely rustles
Amber eyes blazing like fire
Tail whipping from side to side
Rasping tongue licking furry lips
Long delicate whiskers trembling -
A flash of fur, an elegant leap
The kitten pounces on the butterfly . . .
And then falls over.

Ellie Martin (11)
Newport Girls' High School, Newport

Home Is . . .

Home is . . . in the heart of the rainforest,
Where cheeky monkeys hang around.
Home is . . . in a deep, dark, dooming burrow,
Where timid rabbits hide underground.

Home is . . . in an ocean, bottomless and blue,
Where darting fish are free and alone.
Home is . . . in a vast empty savannah,
Where fierce lions stalk and roam.

Home is . . . in the bitter Antarctica,
Where penguins hug and huddle.
Home is . . . in a welcoming special den,
Where bear cubs give a cuddle.

Home is . . . in the splashing stream,
Where otters play and fight.
Home is . . . in a bat's cave,
Where there is hardly any light.

Home is . . . in a torn up box,
Where whining puppies moan and groan.
Home is . . . in a warm, welcoming house,
Where it is right to say home sweet home.

Laura Newey (11)
Newport Girls' High School, Newport

Is Your Little Sister Annoying?

Is your little sister annoying?
Outside my home she is good as gold,
On the inside though a whole new story is told,
She takes my things without asking me,
She gets me into trouble then laughs, 'Hee, hee, hee.'

Is your little sister annoying?
You're probably thinking yes she is,
But she is nothing compared to my little sis,
At school she is little miss perfect, all sweet and kind,
My friends think she's cute, are they blind?

Is your little sister annoying?
Yes she's cute, yes she's sweet,
Yes she's pretty and petite,
None of this matters when she's at home,
Where do people get the idea she's as quiet as a garden gnome?

Is your little sister annoying?
She drives me barmy, she drives me nuts,
Have you ever wondered why I'm covered in cuts?
'She pushed me over,' I tell my mum.
My mum asks, 'Did you?' But she stands there looking dumb.

Although she can be annoying,
Although she can be weird,
Overall I wouldn't change a thing,
I love my little alien sibling!

Holly Davies (11)
Newport Girls' High School, Newport

Home

It's as grand as a palace,
As cosy as a blanket.
My relaxing haven,
I couldn't live without it!
The day we moved in,
It was my brother's birthday,
It's pinned in my brain,
Like it was yesterday!
My bedroom's my sanctuary,
It's a chilling duck egg-blue,
It's been revamped
So everything's pretty new!
Every morning I wake up,
Looking when the sun will rise,
It shines through my bedroom window
And it hurts my sleep-filled eyes.
I will brush my teeth
And quickly dress,
Then my mum will shout,
'Your room's a mess!'
But when I'm off to school,
For yet another day,
I really miss my house
While I'm away!

Phoebe Kynaston (11)
Newport Girls' High School, Newport

Home

My home is like a farmyard filled with animals.
My home is as messy as a pigsty, at least that's what Mum says.
My home is as fun as a circus, my sister is the clown.
My home is like a sparkling paradise, polished to perfection.
My home is like where the monkeys have their tea party;
The place is always a mess.
My home is full of dog hair; I look like a hairy monster.
My home is like an electric reserve,
It's sad to think of the polar bears we could be saving, but aren't.
My home is like a hotel for pets, my mum runs Telford Pet Services.
My home smells as yummy as a restaurant, what's for tea I wonder.
My home is like a school, I'm always being taught.
My home is the best home ever, no matter what it is.
I love my home because home is where the heart is.

Jasmin Walsh (11)
Newport Girls' High School, Newport

Home Sweet Home . . .

Home is more than bricks and stone,
Home is in the heart!
Home is a place where you love and care.

Home could be a caravan,
Home could be a tree,
Home could be for you and me.

Home is a place for you to be free,
Home is a place for you to live,
Home is whatever you want it to be!

Home sweet home!

Rachel Dear (12)
Newport Girls' High School, Newport

Home

Home is where I love to be,
There's five of us in our family.
My puppy, Lottie, excited to play,
As I arrive home after a tiring day.
Round the garden, she chases me,
Past the greenhouse, round the huge beech tree.
Then back inside for a drink and cake,
My favourite chocolate one, I love to bake.

Now up the stairs, two at a time,
Singing as I go, a silly rhyme.
My bedroom on the top floor, a bit of a mess,
My CDs, make-up and my new dress.
My uniform abandoned over the chair,
My comfortable clothes, a quick brush of my hair.
Curled up on the bed, a book in my hand,
My iPod playing my favourite band.

Mum shouts for tea, I rush downstairs,
Round the table, a meal to share.
Then homework and perhaps a little TV,
X Factor, a programme I wanted to see.
Teeth cleaning, I'm ready for bed,
A big cosy duvet, pillows to rest my head.
Home is that special place, I love to be,
With all that is a part of me.

Katy Thorneycroft (11)
Newport Girls' High School, Newport

My House And Me

Here comes another day,
As I open the door to the kitchen.
With the smell of cakes around me,
Food, food is all I can see.
Apart from my mum who's cooking dinner,
Mmmm, my favourite, a prizewinner.

After I've eaten I go into the garden,
Full with woodpeckers and hedgehogs I have to pardon.
As the scampering squirrels scuttle by,
A bird sings a tuneful cry.

I decide to go to the lounge next.
Where what's in front of me is a TV,
As I stand there I am a statue you see.
This is the heart of the house,
Where everyone's equal, even the mouse.

As the night draws near,
I am getting sleepy you hear.
Time to get in my bed,
To lay down my head.
Goodnight,
Sleep tight!

Rebecca Jade Hicks (11)
Newport Girls' High School, Newport

Shadow City

The ruins cold, the fog is deep
In the shadows, young girl creeps.
The statues old, inhabitants fled
None remain, all long-time dead.

In the courtyard, flagstones cracked
Gnarled tree trunks, rotted black.
The royal temple, deserted now
Still stands tall, imposing, proud.

Yet beneath the skeletal leaves
Of the once-lush orchard, a legend breathes.
It watched this civilisation wither
With eyes of lilac, burnished heather.

Long has it been since he last did glide
With wings the size of mountainsides
And claws of ivory, and its teeth
Are like swords without a sheath.

With mighty horns, tail bristles with spikes
Cooled by the air in the pitch-black night.
Its body draped in armoured scales
It dwarfs the mighty humpback whale.

The chant lost when the city fell
Is spoken by this curious girl:
'Serpent of the shadows deep
If thou wake or if thou sleep
Arise once more and feel the breeze
Serpent, serpent, come to me.'

Elri Vaughan (12)
Newport Girls' High School, Newport

The Dance Studio

It's Saturday morning and the dancers arrive,
Armed with shoes, tights, legwarmers and leotards galore.
My senses stir and waken now the music can be heard,
My steps begin to quicken as I burst through the big wooden door.

It's all that stands between me and my chance to feel alive!
'Keep it light!' the teacher shouts
As the deafening noise below
Is one of charging elephants who feel like fairies I have no doubt!

They are the senior ballerinas,
We admire the most their flickering feet
As they glide upon their tippy toes
Unaware of the splintering floorboards beneath.

It's my turn now, I put on my shoes
And fumble with the crisscross silken ties.
Class begins and I take myself to another world.
'Zzzzip that tummy in!' our inspiring teacher cries.

I try my best, I work so hard
To do my perfect pirouettes and pose turns.
That flow gracefully and show my elegant style . . .
But oh my feet - they really burn!

Amber Clark (11)
Newport Girls' High School, Newport

My Home

My home, what a place,
But where can I begin?
There's my mum, my dad, my brother and me,
We sing in the shower,
Fight over remotes,
Plead Mum for gifts,
Make a scene in the shops,
I wouldn't get comfy,
It never stops!
From roast dinner to sausages,
Takeaways too,
We all eat together in our dining room,
My mum does the cleaning, loves to shop,
My dad does the cooking, vegetables he chops,
My home is the best place to be,
Because we all live together as a happy family.

Molly Goulson (11)
Newport Girls' High School, Newport

An Acrostic Poem

A nts live in enormous groups, helping each other to survive,
N ewts are so minute with black spotted tails.

A ardvarks eat all day sucking up all the juicy ants,
C amels have two bumps covering their backs,
R hinos charge very rapidly, pounding the ground so hard,
O ctopuses have eight legs and deadly black ink,
S eal pups have pure white fur, then to grey or brown,
T igers are the biggest cat of four, their stripes are so unique,
I guanas have tails that never end, so curly and so spiky,
C louded leopards are like sly foxes, ambushing their prey.

P enguins survive the freezing conditions of Antarctica,
O wls can't move their eyes, but are still watchful as can be.
E lephants' trunks as flexible as rubber, their tusks as strong as steel,
M eerkats rely on each other, they all have different jobs.

Ellie Paul (11)
Newport Girls' High School, Newport

The Dark Rose

Let the dark rose rise within you as I say my last goodbye,
No tears do I want or do I wish you to cry.

Let the last leaf fall down to the floor,
My life, my heart, my soul are no more.

You don't need me, you have your friends and family too,
Just please remember I'll always love you.

There is no need to say goodbye,
I will see you again one day in the sky.

The biggest star shining so bright,
That will be me at a towering height.

Let the dark rose rise within you as I say my last goodbye,
No tears do I want or do I wish you to cry.

Let the last leaf fall down to the floor,
My life, my heart, my soul are no more.

Maisie Sayers [12]
Newport Girls' High School, Newport

The White Knuckle Ride

Shaking you enter,
With fear in your heart,
You slowly climb in,
Scared as a mouse,
You grip to the handlebars
And hear a faint screech,
The time has come.

Slowly, slowly you creep up,
Your breath held in anticipation,
Here it comes, the big drop,
The white knuckle ride,
A swoop, a scream,
Your pulse is racing,
You feel as though your heart might explode.

Terrified as ever,
Your breath left behind,
You feel a chill,
Crawl up your spine,
A sudden stop
And then the end,
You walk off shaking,
Never again.

Elenor Sims [11]
Newport Girls' High School, Newport

Ode To Home

Oh, home you are a brain,
My shelter from the rain,
Storing memories from over the years,
Fun, excitement and tears.

Oh, home your walls are a skull,
Without you, my life would be dull,
You provide protection at night,
Warmth, comfort and light.

Oh, home, you would not be,
Without a family,

To me, you'd just be a shell.

Chumani Ward (12)
Newport Girls' High School, Newport

Featured Poets:
DEAD POETS
AKA Mark Grist & MC Mixy

Mark Grist and MC Mixy joined forces to become the 'Dead Poets' in 2008.

Since then Mark and Mixy have been challenging the preconceptions of poetry and hip hop across the country. As 'Dead Poets', they have performed in venues ranging from nightclubs to secondary schools; from festivals to formal dinners. They've appeared on Radio 6 Live with Steve Merchant, they've been on a national tour with Phrased and Confused and debuted their show at the 2010 Edinburgh Fringe, which was a huge success.

Both Mark and Mixy work on solo projects as well as working together as the 'Dead Poets'. Both have been Peterborough's Poet Laureate, with Mixy holding the title for 2010.

The 'Dead Poets' are available for workshops in your school as well as other events. Visit www.deadpoetry.co.uk for further information and to contact the guys!

Read on to pick up some fab writing tips!

Your WORKSHOPS

In these Workshops we are going to look at writing styles and examine some literary techniques that the 'Dead Poets' use. Grab a pen, and let's go!

Rhythm Workshop

Rhythm in writing is like the beat in music. Rhythm is when certain words are produced more forcefully than others, and may be held for longer duration. The repetition of a pattern is what produces a 'rhythmic effect'. The word rhythm comes from the Greek meaning of 'measured motion'.

Count the number of syllables in your name. Then count the number of syllables in the following line, which you write in your notepad: 'My horse, my horse, will not eat grass'.

Now, highlight the longer sounding syllables and then the shorter sounding syllables in a different colour.

Di dum, di dum, di dum, di dum is a good way of summing this up.

You should then try to write your own lines that match this rhythm. You have one minute to see how many you can write!

Examples include:
'My cheese smells bad because it's hot'
and
'I do not like to write in rhyme'.

For your poem, why don't you try to play with the rhythm? Use only longer beats or shorter beats? Create your own beat and write your lines to this?

Rhyme Workshop

Start off with the phrase 'I'd rather be silver than gold' in your notepad. and see if you can come up with lines that rhyme with it -
'I'd rather have hair than be bald'
'I'd rather be young than be old'
'I'd rather be hot than cold'
'I'd rather be bought than sold'

Also, pick one of these words and see how many rhymes you can find:

Rose

Wall

Warm

Danger

What kinds of rhymes did you come up with? Are there differences in rhymes? Do some words rhyme more cleanly than others? Which do you prefer and why?

Lists Workshop

Game - you (and you can ask your friends or family too) to write as many reasons as possible for the following topics:

Annoying things about siblings

The worst pets ever

The most disgusting ingredients for a soup you can think of

Why not try writing a poem with the same first 2, 3 or 4 words?

I am ...

Or

I love it when ...

Eg:

I am a brother

I am a listener

I am a collector of secrets

I am a messer of bedrooms.

Onomatopoeia Workshop

Divide a sheet of A4 paper into 8 squares.

You then have thirty seconds to draw/write what could make the following sounds:

Splash	Ping
Drip	Bang
Rip	Croak
Crack	Splash

Now try writing your own ideas of onomatopoeia. Why might a writer include onomatopoeia in their writing?

Repetition Workshop

Come up with a list of words/ phrases, aim for at least 5. You now must include one of these words in your piece at least 6 times. You aren't allowed to place these words/ phrases at the beginning of any of the lines.

Suggested words/phrases:

Why

Freedom

Laughing

That was the best day ever

I can't find the door

I'm in trouble again

The best

Workshop
POETRY 101

Below is a poem written especially for Poetry Matters, by MC Mixy.
Why not try and write some more poems of your own?

What is Matter?
© MC Mixy

What matters to me may not be the same things that matter to you
You may not agree with my opinion mentality or attitude
The order in which I line up my priorities to move
Choose to include my view and do what I do due to my mood
And state of mind
I make the time to place the lines on stacks of paper and binds
Concentrate on my artwork hard I can't just pass and scrape behind
Always keep close mates of mine that make things right
And even those who can't … just cos I love the way they can try
What matters to me is doing things the right way
It's tough this game of life we play what we think might stray from what others might say
In this world of individuality we all wanna bring originality
Live life and drift through casually but the vicious reality is
Creativity is unique
Opinions will always differ but if you figure you know the truth, speak
So many things matter to me depending on how tragically deep you wanna go
I know I need to defy gravity on this balance beam
As I laugh and breathe draft and read map the scene practise piece smash the beat and graphic release
Visual and vocal it's a standard procedure
Have to believe and don't bite the hand when it feeds ya

If you wanna be a leader you need to stay out of the pen where the sheep
are
The things that matter to me are
My art and my friends
That will stay from the start to the end
People will do things you find hard to amend
Expect the attacks and prepare you gotta be smart to defend
I put my whole heart in the blend the mass is halved yet again
I'm marked by my pen a big fish fighting sharks of men
In a small pond
Dodging harpoons and nets hooks and predators tryna dismember ya
I won't let them I won't get disheartened I can fend for myself
As long as I'm doing what's important
I'm my mind where I'm supported is a just cause to be supporting
In these appalling hard times I often find myself falling when
Only two aspects of my life keep me sane and allow me to stand tall again
Out of all of them two is a small number
It's a reminder I remind ya to hold necessity and let luxury fall under
Try to avoid letting depression seep through
Take the lesson we actually need a lot less than we think we do
So what matters to you?
They may be similar to things that matter to me
I'm actually lacking the need of things I feel would help me to succeed
Though I like to keep it simple, I wanna love, I wanna breed
I'm one of many individuals in this world where importance fluctuates and
varies
Things that matter will come and go
But the ones that stay for long enough must be worth keeping close
If you're not sure now don't watch it you'll know when you need to know
Me, I think I know now … yet I feel and fear I don't.

Turn overleaf for a poem by Mark Grist
and some fantastic hints and tips!

Workshop
POETRY 101

What Tie Should I Wear Today?

© Mark Grist

I wish I had a tie that was suave and silk and slick,
One with flair, that's debonair and would enchant with just one flick,
Yeah, I'd like that … a tie that's hypnotizing,
I'd be very restrained and avoid womanising,
But all the lady teachers would still say 'Mr Grist your tie's so charming!'
As I cruise into their classrooms with it striking and disarming.
At parents' evenings my tie's charm would suffice,
In getting mums to whisper as they leave 'Your English teacher seems nice!'

Or maybe an evil-looking tie - one that's the business,
Where students will go 'Watch out! Mr Grist is
on the prowl with that evil tie.'
The one that cornered Josh and then ripped out his eye.
Yeah no one ever whispers, no one ever sniggers,
Or my tie would rear up and you'd wet your knickers.
Maybe one girl just hasn't heard the warning,
Cos she overslept and turned up late to school that morning,
And so I'd catch her in my lesson yawning … oh dear.
I'd try to calm it down, but this tie's got bad ideas.
It'd size the girl up and then just as she fears,
Dive in like a serpent snapping at her ears.
There'd be a scream, some blood and lots and lots of tears,
And she wouldn't be able to yawn again for years.

Or maybe … a tie that everyone agrees is mighty fine
And people travel from miles around to gawp at the design
I'd like that … a tie that pushes the boundaries of tieware right up to the limit
It'd make emos wipe their tears away while chavs say 'It's wicked innit?'
and footy lads would stop me with 'I'd wear that if I ever won the cup.'
And I'd walk through Peterborough to slapped backs, high fives, thumbs up
While monosyllabic teenagers would just stand there going 'Yup.'

I don't know. I'd never be sure which of the three to try
As any decision between them would always end a tie.

Tips and Advice for
PERFORMING
Your Poem

So you've written your poem, now how about performing it.
Whether you read your poem for the first time in front of your class, school
or strangers at an open mic event or poetry slam, these tips will help you
make the best of your performance.

Breathe and try to relax.

Every poet that reads in front of people for the first time feels a bit nervous,
when you're there you are in charge and nothing serious can go wrong.

People at poetry slams or readings are there to support the poets. They really are!

**If you can learn your poem off by heart that is brilliant, however having a piece of paper or
notebook with your work in is fine, though try not to hide behind these.**

It's better to get some eye contact with the audience.
If you're nervous find a friendly face to focus on.

Try to read slowly and clearly and enjoy your time in the spotlight.

**Don't rush up to the microphone, make sure it's at the right height for you and if you need
it adjusted ask one of the team around you.**

Before you start, stand up as straight as you can and get your body as
comfortable as you can and remember to hold your head up.

The microphone can only amplify what what's spoken into it; if you're very loud you might
end up deafening people and if you only whisper or stand too far away you won't be heard.

**When you say something before your poem, whether that's hello or just the title of your
poem, try and have a listen to how loud you sound. If you're too quiet move closer to the
microphone, if you're too loud move back a bit.**

Remember to breathe! Don't try to say your poem so quickly you can't find
time to catch your breath.

And finally, **enjoy!**

Poetry FACTS

Here are a selection of fascinating poetry facts!

No word in the English language rhymes with 'MONTH'.

William Shakespeare was born on 23rd April 1564 and died on 23rd April 1616.

The haiku is one of the shortest forms of poetic writing.
Originating in Japan, a haiku poem is only seventeen syllables, typically broken down into three lines of five, seven and five syllables respectively.

The motto of the Globe Theatre was 'totus mundus agit histrionem' (the whole world is a playhouse).

The Children's Laureate award was an idea by Ted Hughes and Michael Morpurgo.

The 25th January each year is Burns' Night, an occasion in honour of Scotland's national poet Robert Burns.

Spike Milligan's 'On the Ning Nang Nong' was voted the UK's favourite comic poem in 1998.

Did you know *onomatopoeia* means the word you use sounds like the word you are describing – like the rain *pitter-patters* or the snow *crunches* under my foot.

'Go' is the shortest complete sentence in the English language.

Did you know rhymes were used in olden days to help people remember the news? Ring-o'-roses is about the Plague!

The Nursery Rhyme 'Old King Cole' is based on a real king and a real historical event. King Cole is supposed to have been an actual monarch of Britain who ruled around 200 A.D.

Edward Lear popularised the limerick with his poem 'The Owl and the Pussy-Cat'.

Lewis Carroll's poem 'The Jabberwocky' is written in nonsense style.

> POEM – noun
>
> 1. a composition in verse, esp. one that is characterized by a highly developed artistic form and by the use of heightened language and rhythm to express an intensely imaginative interpretation of the subject.

Poetry TIPS

We have compiled some helpful tips for you budding poets...

In order to write poetry, read lots of poetry!

Keep a notebook with you at all times so you can write whenever (and wherever) inspiration strikes.

Every line of a poem should be important to the poem and interesting to read. A poem with only 3 great lines should be 3 lines long.

Use an online rhyming dictionary to improve your vocabulary.

Use free workshops and help sheets to learn new poetry styles.

Experiment with visual patterns - does your written poetry create a good pattern on the page?

Try to create pictures in the reader's mind - aim to fire the imagination.

Develop your voice. Become comfortable with how you write.

Listen to criticism, and try to learn from it, but don't live or die by it.

Say what you want to say, let the reader decide what it means.

Notice what makes other's poetry memorable. Capture it, mix it up and make it your own. (Don't copy other's work word for word!)

Go wild. Be funny. Be serious. Be whatever you want!

Grab hold of something you feel - anything you feel - and write it.

The more you write, the more you develop. Write poetry often.

Use your imagination, your own way of seeing.

Feel free to write a bad poem, it will develop your 'voice'.

Did you know ...?

'The Epic of Gilgamesh' was written thousands of years ago in Mesopotamia and is the oldest poem on record.

Wordsmith

The *premier* magazine
for creative young people

A platform for your imagination and creativity. Showcase your ideas and have your say. Welcome to a place where like-minded young people express their personalities and individuality knows no limits.

For further information visit *www.youngwriters.co.uk*.

A peek into Wordsmith world ...

Poetry and Short Stories
We feature both themed and non-themed work every issue. Previous themes have included; dreams and aspirations, superhero stories and ghostly tales.

Next Generation Author
This section devotes two whole pages to one of our readers' work. The perfect place to showcase a selection of your poems, stories or both!

Guest Author Features & Workshops
Interesting and informative tutorials on different styles of poetry and creative writing. Famous authors and illustrators share their advice with us on how to create gripping stories and magical picturebooks. Novelists like Michael Morpurgo and Celia Rees go under the spotlight to answer our questions.

The fun doesn't stop there ...
Every issue we tell you what events are coming up across the country. We keep you up to date with the latest film and book releases and we feature some yummy recipes to help feed the brain and get the creative juices flowing.

So with all this and more, Wordsmith is *the* magazine to be reading.

If you are too young for Wordsmith magazine or have a younger friend who enjoys creative writing, then check out Scribbler!. Scribbler! is for 7-11 year-olds and is jam-packed full of brilliant features, young writers' work, competitions and interviews too. For further information check out *www.youngwriters.co.uk* or ask an adult to call us on (01733) 890066.

To get an adult to subscribe to either magazine for you,
ask them to visit the website or give us a call.

Another Day

Another day, another way,
Another time to wait.

My life always flashes before my eyes,
With all the lies you tell me over and over again,
It cuts deep like a knife inside,
Sometimes I feel I could just die.

Motivation, movement, motion.
Still, stable and stolen.
You stole from me my life, my soul and my heart,
I thought you had fallen from the sky to save me,
But instead you enslaved me.

Likes flies to a web,
Likes bees to a flower,
You took my power.

Sometimes I sit glaring out the window
Watching the world pass me by.
I just want to be able to fly
Get away from the hurt and pain
You made me . . .

Ashliegh Davidson (17)
Rutland County College, Oakham

Mid-Week Dinner

Can't understand people who do things by the book.
Few pleasures in life are greater than throwing in
a bit of this, a bit of that,
a pinch of curiosity
and limitless endeavour to shock, surprise, entice
your guests and the ultimate judge:
yourself
delight your taste buds with spices and deny
all logical reasoning and just
improvise.

Emily-Jayne Shell (18)
Rutland County College, Oakham

A Lost Face . . .

Walking down the road I see a pretty face
One that I know but could never replace
I hope she doesn't realise that I'm right over here
Should I start running and should I just go?

She keeps on following; I've got nowhere to go
And she seems to catch me wherever I may roam
I've got no idea where I should be going
As long as I'm being chased by this pretty woman

You might think this is good but you should really know
That in fact it's ghastly and it's oh so wrong

I want to know where you are going
I want to know where you have been
I want to see you face again
But I really don't know when.

Ben Harris (17)
Rutland County College, Oakham

Four Seasons

You are my everything,
my every day of fun.
The snow at Christmas,
the frost from a morning run.

You are my everything,
the birds in the sky.
The bright summer sun,
you made me fly.

You are my everything,
the angel's song.
The fall of autumn leaves,
never leave me for long.

You are my everything,
a perfect piece of art.
The lambs in spring,
I give you my heart.

Murray Watkins (16)
Rutland County College, Oakham

Nine Statement Pieces

Thick, gold in colour, snake skin effect.
The next one is smaller; brown, white and green bands streak across it.
Following that, a thin gold band, painted with white, green and pink flowers.
To finish, four plain gold bands.

Red chunky cubes wrap around my arm, attached together with light blue beads.
The next are pretty plain. Black, blue, pink and green beads.
Then pure purple.
Then silver
And finally,
Black.

Niki Brown (18)
Rutland County College, Oakham

In Flanders Field

In Flanders fields where they lay
The poppies grow and dance all day
The generation that stood and fell
So that kings could be in marble

They lie with their brothers
And letters from mothers
Like logs stacked on each other
In a field that no one knows today

They thought it would be over
But never did they come through Dover

So they lie there for us
Waiting for the end
Of what they saw the start of
And the pleasure of our company
To join them so that
They can say
In remembrance.

Jonathan Tyler (17)
Rutland County College, Oakham

Lust

It felt as smooth as a velvet rose
I felt small tingles within my toes
The hairs on my neck flared upwards like fire
Body filled with lust and pure desire

It started off slowly and then became faster
Little did I know what was going to happen after
I was overcome with a sense of love
Felt I was flying through the skies like a beautiful white dove

With little expectation he pulled away
Come forwards again is what I wanted to say
I felt a punch within my heart
I thought this would be the beginning of a new start

Days passed and nothing came of what went on
It's almost invisible an end of a song
I didn't think I would be in pain like this
At the end of the day I have to remember, it was only a kiss.

Charlotte Croxall (16)
Rutland County College, Oakham

Broken Breaks

A time in my life,
When everything is coming my way -
I'm in the wrong lane.

That's what I get for taking advice
And taking a car,
With a rag-tag steering wheel

And broken brakes.
The windows are smashed,
The body splattered, crushed;

It isn't changing
And the bolts are shifting.
The battered box creaks at the wheels,

The doors have come away.
Nuts and bolts undoing, all unscrewing,
The seats behind me burning -

And I'm just driving along;
Against the river of the road,
Swimming upstream like a salmon.

The engine is growling,
Hungry again. Insatiable thirst:
Petrol patters, pours from the roof,

Windscreen wipers whisper,
Polish away the gurning storm
And sour, scowling sun.

The cracks are forming -
The engines are rumbling,
Hungry, hungry. The smouldering seats

And blazing still,
Cackling at my misfit car,
Driving up the wrong damn lane.

Robyn Benedikz (16)
Rutland County College, Oakham

My Cat

I once had a lazy fat black cat
He lazed around on the fluffy black mat
Until one day
He went outside to play
His black mat went up in a blaze
As all I could do was stare and gaze
I could not understand how this could be
All I could do was run and flee
He must have been dead
With body now separated from head
I could barely blink
My heart now starting to sink
I will now purchase a frog
It better not fall down the bog.

Ryan Dalby (16)
Rutland County College, Oakham

The Sea

A shimmering sapphire shining bright,
Beneath a diamond encrusted night.
The constant movement of the sea,
Is home to the fish, wild and free.

This wonder of nature is so special,
As the sound upon the pebble.
When wave breaks its destructive power,
Shows no mercy and will devour.

As a new day begins,
The story is forgotten.
As the grey skies clear
And become clouds of cotton.

Tayla Bates (12)
St Dominic's High School for Girls, Brewood

Home

Ah, sweet land of my birth!
Grandparents waving from their door.
Even Grandpa was moist-eyed.
The farewell party with my friends
Bittersweet fun.

Longed for foods;
The conveyer belt of delights in the
Kaiten sushi shop circling endlessly round,
When my mother was too tired to cook.
The Yakiniku shop's thick steaks
Sizzling sweetly on the griddle.

A grumbling stomach on the way home
From abacus class filled with a steaming dumpling.
Udon noodles in a miso broth,
An egg cracked into it to cook - steaming heaven.

The thirty minute amble to school with Masami and Chiharu.
Finds along the way, stubborn silence after a spat.
School bags; red for girls and black for boys,
Almost bigger than me.
What a weight!

Ah, Grandma, Grandpa!
Only another year and a half and I'll be home!

Shiori Harada (12)
St Dominic's High School for Girls, Brewood

This Poem Will Live Forever

Ebony, she's crazy but sweet,
Her favourite thing to do is eat.
The only one that belongs to me,
Take a guess it's my dear Charli.
Hexi, the little witch,
But if cuteness were money she'd be rich.
Scamp, for her, luck comes in the ton
And to be around she's loads of fun.
Peter Pan is cute and tiny,
After he's groomed his coat is so shiny.
Cookie a fluffy, dun pony,
A fjord but not the only.
Toffee is a fjord as well,
There are lots because they school so well.
The last is Truffle, the little baby
And he'll school one day, maybe.
Animals of all types I adore,
I could write down a million more.
The moral of this story is that pets' lives go fast
And unfortunately they just don't last.
My poem is about to stop but the meaning never,
So here's the end and that's forever.

Caitlin Beaumont (12)
St Dominic's High School for Girls, Brewood

Autumn

Autumn is here,
Birds tweet, tweet, tweet,
Gushing winds blow,
While the leaves flutter to the floor.

The bare trees sway,
Animals rush for hibernation,
Beautiful leaves float,
Side to side.

The dewy green grass,
Covered in rusty coloured leaves,
There is silence,
The whistling wind slows.

Dark nights draw near,
Cold, cold days and nights,
As we say goodbye to colourful autumn,
The dreaded winter begins.

Emily Heath (12)
St Dominic's High School for Girls, Brewood

Summer

S un shining brightly
U tterly gorgeous sometimes
M usic playing in a quiet field
M uch to people's delight a red sky at night
E veryone having a laugh
R eally cheerful until the end.

Andi Hickey (11)
St Dominic's High School for Girls, Brewood

Halloween

H aving a fun time trick or treating
A waking bats high in the trees
L ighting the candles to put inside the pumpkin
L icking all the Halloween lollipops
O wls flying across the moon
W itches coming to your door
E ating pumpkin pie
E njoying dressing up
N ever-ending amounts of children in costumes.

Rebecca Bodger (11)
St Dominic's High School for Girls, Brewood

Life Is Family

L ove family forever and on.
I never want to give up!
F orever blooming with kindness.
E very day's a new chapter.

I s a flame of peace.
S ometimes evil!

F orgetful.
A bubble around me!
M e and my family.
I llness.
L ove your joy.
Y our understanding is my love.

Georgina Hicken (11)
St Dominic's High School for Girls, Brewood

Figure Skating

I really love to figure skate
And sing and dance and stay up late
But when I have nothing to do
My mum calls me 'Grumpy Moo'!

Jessica Randle (13)
St Dominic's High School for Girls, Brewood

Me!

I am a monkey swinging from a treetop,
I am a big friendly giant, not really,
I am a funny poodle walking on the beach,
I am a colourful lizard when I am happy.

I am a rain cloud when I am sad,
I am the colour red when I am angry,
I am energetic when I play sports,
I am just me!

Emily Atkinson (11)
St Dominic's High School for Girls, Brewood

Leah

L eaves falling from the trees
E ggs, chocolate eggs in spring, yummy
A little sun that is all we need in summer but we never get it
H ooray, winter's here, it's my birthday.

Leah Moogan (11)
St Dominic's High School for Girls, Brewood

Hannah

H annah's smile keeps me going all day long
A nd she's athletic, she can run like the wind.
N othing that she does is ever naughty.
N ice as can be, she will cheer you up.
A lso she is kind in every possible way.
H annah is like a cute, cuddly teddy bear.

Holly Hagan (11)
St Dominic's High School for Girls, Brewood

The Night Sky

The sun says goodbye
Only to say hello again
So we can see the star twinkle
Brightly in the night sky.

There are unknown things in this world
That even the scientists can't recall.
They look up in their telescopes
And say, 'Could there be more?'

The people wake up to go to their busy jobs
As the stars are among us,
But we cannot see them with our eyes
And it takes us with surprise.

Maiya Grant (11)
St Dominic's High School for Girls, Brewood

Lonely

All alone,
Thinking your life's at end,
As gloomy as a thundercloud,
With no friend.

Feeling neglected and worried,
With a cold tear on my face,
I'm forgotten forever,
And walking in a slow rejected pace.

With no happiness to live with,
And feeling so lost,
I may not be happy again,
I'm as cold as frost.

Grace Ripalo (12)
St Dominic's High School for Girls, Brewood

The Sea

The sea can be a strange, blue Powerade drink,
It can be an angry tiger,
Pawing at the cliffs.
The sea is a playground for all
The fish and children,
But it can be a blueberry milkshake
All mixed up and shaken.

The sea is a thirsty dog, lapping up the sand
But when you see the ginormous waves,
Beware of its dark blue hand.
The sea is a nature reserve for all the animals
And the black clouds are God's hands,
Controlling an angry bull.

So the sea is a blue duvet covering up the land,
But it can be a calm cat, sleeping on the sand.

Imogen Bebb (11)
St Dominic's High School for Girls, Brewood

A Friend

A friend is like a brand new gate
That never comes unlatched.
A friend is like a ghost,
Whose spirit never dies.
A friend is forever
So never leave their side.

Rebecca Evans (11)
St Dominic's High School for Girls, Brewood

Midnight

The clock struck twelve,
As she stared at the pearly white moon,
She crept,
Into the deep dark depth,
She heard a horrific scream,
The adrenaline rushing through her veins,
The frost on the window panes.

Her ankle gave way and came down with a thud,
Her head trickled with blood,
Right in front of her did lay a gravestone,
Engraved with her name and RIP.

That night in the graveyard,
Scared her for life!

Savannah Kitson (11)
St Dominic's High School for Girls, Brewood

Potatoes

They are brown and round
And found
In the ground.

With the slugs
And snails all around.

But when you dig them
Out of the ground,
They are delicious
All the way round.

Ellena Thomas (13)
St Dominic's High School for Girls, Brewood

The Seasons

Leaves, leaves on the trees,
Yellow and brown like the colour of bees.
Push them round and into a mound
Or watch them drifting to the ground.

Lambs playing in the field,
Farmers inside eating soup.
The flowers are springing, opening up,
Even the little yellow buttercups.

On the beach, in the sea,
There's fish, sharks and seaweed.
Building sandcastles lots of fun,
Whilst singing along to hot cross buns.

Build a snowman or have a snow fight,
Or put some snow down my brother's top, I think I just might.
Wrap up our scarves, put on our gloves
And drink hot chocolate which everyone loves.

Reece Billen (12)
St Dominic's High School for Girls, Brewood

My Family

M ost important people you will know
Y our family are watching you as you grow

F avourite people on the Earth
A unties, uncles, nans and granddads love right from birth
M om and Dad are the best
I believe that but they think I'm a pest
L ove comes from all of them
Y ou will see that now and then.

Hannah-Mae Prodger (12)
St Dominic's High School for Girls, Brewood

Me

I am funny like a clown
But never in my life down.
People say I am loveable,
But most of the time I am just gullible.

My life is like a story
And filled with lots of glory.
Adventures catch my eye,
But sometimes I get bored and sigh.

When I get tired and go to bed,
I have been known to have said,
That I am the best and no one knows why,
I sleep, walk and talk until I will die.

Ella Jones (11)
St Dominic's High School for Girls, Brewood

Cleopatra's Moon

I sit, I stare, I wait . . .
In the darkness there's always light.
Looking across a luminous sea you always find life.
You never really understand what's important unless you look up.
Beauty has many names always changing
But there's always one type of beauty for you and me . . .
The moon.
We sit, we stare, we wait.

Cleopatra Darwish (12)
St Dominic's High School for Girls, Brewood

Splish, Splash, Splosh

Splish, splash, splosh,
People saying oh gosh!

Splosh, splish, splash,
Legs kicking with a crash!

Splash, splosh, splish,
In the water like a fish!

Splish, splash, splosh,
Swimming is my passion,
As you can see,
I swim day and night,
It's all about *me.*

Emma Hudson (12)
St Dominic's High School for Girls, Brewood

What Is Important To Me?

Pandora bracelet,
Silver, metal, shiny,
Full of charms,
Of all kinds,
Different sizes,
Different shapes,
Each with their own meaning.

Kelly Anne Westwood (13)
St Dominic's High School for Girls, Brewood

Chocolate!

Chocolate is nice,
Chocolate is sweet,
Chocolate is something that I like to eat.

Chocolate is swirly,
Chocolate is straight,
Chocolate is sometimes served on a plate.

Chocolate is cold,
Chocolate is hot,
Chocolate, well I like it a lot.

Chocolate is hard,
Chocolate is chewy,
My brother says that chocolate is gooey.

So as you can see,
I like chocolate a lot,
Especially the hot stuff served in a pot.

Poppy Virgina Mollie Thompson (12)
St Dominic's High School for Girls, Brewood

Harvest

The trees are set ablaze with colour
And the fields are a vast swathe of gold.
As autumn takes over from summer,
The days get dark and cold.

The farmer works hard on the harvest,
To gather the food that we need
And we should give thanks for his efforts,
For each of us that he will feed.

The harvest is gathered for us to eat,
Corn, barley, oats and wheat.
Crimson apples, russet pears
And purple berries for us to share.

But God gave us the fertile earth,
He made the warming sun
And we give thanks for all we are worth
And praise for all He has done.

Lydia Jones (11)
St Dominic's High School for Girls, Brewood

Seasons

It's spring,
Newborn lambs play,
Yellow daffodils sway,
Trees blossom and grow,
Easter will come and go.

It's summer,
Freshly cut grass,
Long days that pass,
Birds sing without a worry,
Holidays disappear in a hurry.

It's autumn,
Red, yellow, brown and gold,
All these colours warm and bold,
Harvest then Halloween,
Bonfire Night must be seen.

It's winter,
Cold and dark nights,
Are made fun with snowball fights,
Wildlife goes into a deep sleep,
Christmas time is at our feet.

Although the year has gone in a hurry,
The seasons will start again, don't worry.

Emily Mackriel (11)
St Dominic's High School for Girls, Brewood

First Scuba Dive

My eyes wander,
Misty blue depths surround me.
I swim further.
My fluorescent yellow fins glide across the muddy ground,
With BCD in hand I descend further down the darkened edge of the cliff,
Breathing fine,
I check my pressure levels, 200.
I can go on.
I catch my breath quickly as a trout comes flapping past.
It swims across my gloved hand absentmindedly
Looking around I see more in groups.
But I only move forward.
Till the end of the dive.

Katie Randall (13)
St Dominic's High School for Girls, Brewood

Friends

My friends are important to me
Because they see what I see.

All the things I would do to keep us close
As few friends do.

We got to town
We go to the park
And in the summer we have a laugh.

Gemma Webb (12)
Sir Christopher Hatton School, Wellingborough

War

War is a big, disgusting and horrible fight
With all the guns going *bang, bang, bang.*
All the explosives going *bang!*
It goes into the ground.
Then there is a big hole when it goes *bang!*
Some soldiers are dying and also saving others.
You have lots and lots of shine and they whine for me to take them.
We have to stop and then we will have world peace.
Then the world would be silent.
Then that's the end of the wars.

Luke Jordan Abraham (11)
Sir Christopher Hatton School, Wellingborough

Rabbits

Rabbits are fun to play with.
Rabbits are really furry.
Rabbits make everybody feel all hairy.
Rabbits make everybody feel really soft.
Rabbits are always there to cuddle in a storm.
Rabbits cover everybody in lots of hairs.
Rabbits always eat carrots.
Rabbits love to stay in their homes called a rabbit hole.

Emma Teall (11)
Sir Christopher Hatton School, Wellingborough

LUFC

Leeds United is the only team for me
We are not the best side around
But we are okay, believe me
1904 was the year we were found.

We have had our good days and our bad days for years and years
But when Leeds score everybody cheers
So that's why I support the mighty Whites
And will for years and years to come.

Jack Shayler [12]
Sir Christopher Hatton School, Wellingborough

What Matters To Me

Bang! Oh no, here she comes,
All she wants is some fun.
But she can be excited,
Though according to me she can be lively.

Even when she's having dinner,
We still call her a killer.
Thud! The stairs go to signal, she's on her way,
Come on everyone at bay.
My dog Willow matters to me.

Thomas Taylor [11]
Sir Christopher Hatton School, Wellingborough

Animals Matter To Me, Do They Matter To You?

I think animals are cute,
I think animals are sweet,
So why let them get hurt
And help them with me.

I think animals are lively little things,
I think animals are beautiful big things,
The lovely thing about animals
Is they're always there by your side.

Animals will always love you
So can you love them back?
By helping animal shelters
The poor things will live and be okay.

Rachael Lee Guastella (11)
Sir Christopher Hatton School, Wellingborough

Flowers

Some flowers are yellow like the bumblebee
So pretty as can be.

So many colours to choose from
Purple, yellow, pink
Some people say it stinks.

But I do not listen to what they say
Because I always follow my own way
Purple, yellow, pink
That is what I think.

Salma Ali (11)
Sir Christopher Hatton School, Wellingborough

Christmas

C hristmas is my birthday
H o! Ho! Ho!
R eindeer are on their way
I like it!
S uper presents you get
T he best time of the year
M erry Christmas
A Christmas dinner is so nice
S uper fun for everyone.

Jacob Judd (12)
Sir Christopher Hatton School, Wellingborough

Table Tennis

Playing table tennis with my friends
But eventually the game ends.
I say well done then move on
Then I play my next game
Ping pong goes the ball!

I use my forehand
I use my backhand
I'm in the mood
It's time to shine
I'll do fine
I win the game
Ping pong once again.

Stuart Jones (12)
Sir Christopher Hatton School, Wellingborough

My Friends And Family

M y friends and family
Y es it is wonderful

F riends are there for you
R esponsible or non-responsible
I f they fall out they will not shout
E njoy your friendship whilst it lasts
N obody's there for your grasp
D eeds and dares, make sure you're good
S mash goes the window, your friend blames you

F amily is always there
A t a time so bad
M y grandad's gone, time to move on
I f you're there just have fun
L et it be a time to move on
Y ou are big or small, you are part of a family song.

Rickesh Mistry (12)
Sir Christopher Hatton School, Wellingborough

Drinks

How could you live without a drink?
Before you answer, have a think,
It doesn't matter what type of drink,
If it's a liquid like Coke, orange or whatever,
Does it really matter?
No, not really,
As long as it's a drink!

Josh Orry (12)
Sir Christopher Hatton School, Wellingborough

Love Once Lost

He holds her hands tightly
And says he loves her
He whispers in the ear
And says he must go
She hears the train coming
And suddenly starts to hum
To block out the pain of waiting for the train
She hugs him tightly
As the tears roll down her cheek
She puts her head on his shoulder
As her tears start to stain his suit
The train arrives slowly
As he lets her go
He says he will be gone for a year
As he walks to the train slowly
He says something aloud
She doesn't hear so she is left standing there
Love once lost.

Maria Ross (12)
Sir Christopher Hatton School, Wellingborough

Family

F un and games are what my family play
A nd on holidays Nan is there to pay
M y mum is lovely, nice and kind
I 'm sometimes a pain but Mum doesn't mind
L ucky me I have my family
Y oung at heart, Mum, Grandad and Nanny.

Ryan Lack (13)
Sir Christopher Hatton School, Wellingborough

Friends

My friends are my world,
They listen and trust me,
They hug and they love me,
We're really different in every way,
We never fight but sometimes we might
And all I've got to say,
Is that we'll be friends all the way.

Kristina Alice Hughes (12)
Sir Christopher Hatton School, Wellingborough

Man United

Man United are the best,
They're better than the rest,
They're top of the League
And I know they will always be,
They have won lots of trophies,
They have won lots of medals,
They have had the same manager for twenty-eight years,
He's made giants cheer
And he's also made puddles of tears.

John Jo A Kersey (11)
Sir Christopher Hatton School, Wellingborough

Holidays

What matters to me,
Is going on holiday with my family,
The hot weather, how nice!
Plenty of time, relaxing on the beach and by the pool.

Every day there's something to do,
From staying in or going far away.
Even things to do at night,
Go to the local town,
A walk along the beach
And going out for meals.

What matters to me,
Having ice creams in the baking weather.
A hot drink when it goes cold
And doing whatever I want.

What matters to me,
Watching a firework show,
At the end of the summer.
A few days before I leave the campsite
And start my long journey home.

Claire Durkin (12)
Sir Christopher Hatton School, Wellingborough

My House

Homes are vital but some can change,
Living there for eight years, surely that's lots of days!
The bigger the better's not the case,
Or if green or grey's the colour of its face.

Apparently if you live in a better location,
Your house will get a better quotation!
It doesn't matter if mine is rubbish,
It's still on the top of my list!

Ben O'Rourke (11)
Sir Christopher Hatton School, Wellingborough

Ducks

Ducks mean a lot to me!
Ducks are fluffy,
Sometimes even puffy.

Ducks mean a lot to me!
You feed them when you're young,
You have lots of fun.

Ducks mean a lot to me!
They live near the river
Feeding in winter gives me shivers.

Ducks mean a lot to me!
They can fly up to the sky
And say goodbye, *quack.*

Niamh Howes (11)
Sir Christopher Hatton School, Wellingborough

What Matters To Me

What matters to me is animal cruelty,
They're just like us,
They just need more fuss,
You don't need to be cruel to them,
It's not fair,
After all,
They just want someone to be there.

What matters to me is the snow,
You wrap up warm,
Then go out in the storm,
Throwing snowballs,
Then taking a fall,
The snow is slippy
And the wind is nippy,
Just be careful out there
And don't be scared.

What matters to me is music,
Playing the keyboard
And going to lessons that I really enjoy,
I don't know what I want to be,
I guess,
I'll just be me.

Amber Louise Harris (11)
Sir Christopher Hatton School, Wellingborough

As The Tide Left

As the tide left
The sea waved goodbye
And all the waves shimmered
Under the moonlit sky

The stars played games with me
But I couldn't help but cry
Because the sea had left me
And I couldn't figure out why

The sand still felt warm beneath my feet
If I said I was happy that would be a lie
For my darling sea had left me once again
And all I could do was watch the waves die.

Deanna Ellen Jackson (13)
Sir Christopher Hatton School, Wellingborough

Money

What matters to me? Money matters to me.
Money can be your whole life.
Food, drink, games and gifts.
Money is perfect in all different ways
But the only thing money can't buy is . . .
Friendship.

Jack Lawrence (12)
Sir Christopher Hatton School, Wellingborough

The Emotions Of A Goal

Running through the opposition while passing to your teammates.
Skilling everybody up as the keeper anxiously waits.
I've got past everybody now, it's just me and the keeper.
Bang! The ball hits the net,
I never knew he was such a weeper.
Oh my God, I've finally scored,
The cheers and the glory!
The other team with their heads down
Knowing they played so poorly.
This is amazing,
I have actually scored a goal.
This is as important to me as
'Deal Or No Deal' is to Noel!

Troy Franklin (13)
Sir Christopher Hatton School, Wellingborough

Make-Up

Mascara and all the tiaras.
They're just materialistic things.
Make-up is just pasted on your face.
It does not make you unique.
Beauty is on the inside.
Ask yourself, do people treat you the same?

Paige Thoms (12)
Sir Christopher Hatton School, Wellingborough

Leeds United

Leeds United are the best,
They are better than the rest.
They do as best as they can,
Leeds United have a main man.

Leeds United know they're the best,
At people's houses they are the guest.
Schmeichel is a brilliant goalie,
He is like a quick Moley.

Leeds United are the best,
They call their bed their nest.
I love Leeds so much,
No players are Dutch.

Bremner White (12)
Sir Christopher Hatton School, Wellingborough

Art And Crafts

A rts and crafts
R ealistic masterpiece
T akes time.

A nything you want to draw
N o boundaries
D raw day and night.

C reating a piece of art is a delight
R etry to get better
A ny object can be done
F orms of art
T aught at school
S culpting.

Jayden Herring (13)
Sir Christopher Hatton School, Wellingborough

My Pets

My guinea pigs - greedy little things, they eat 24/7.
They love to be stroked, cuddled and loved.
They squeak until they go to sleep, and then they'll wake up
And have a bite to eat.
Those greedy guinea pigs . . .

My rabbits are big and tough but really they are soft inside.
They dig until the day is over, then plot their escape plan.
Once they escaped, but we were on holiday.
Nan to the rescue! She was chasing them round and round
In circles until they went back in the cage.
Once we came home we laughed all day
But who wasn't laughing!
We'll tell that story for days on end . . .

Grace Manning (11)
Sir Christopher Hatton School, Wellingborough

Peace

World peace is what matters to me
I wish it was for them, I wish it was for them
World peace is what matters to me
I wish it was for them

When the world is split in two
And there's nothing we can do
Just turn around and you will find
The world that everyone knew

World peace is what matters to me
I wish it was for them, I wish it was for them
World peace is what matters to me
I wish it was for them.

Lauren Gibbons (11)
Sir Christopher Hatton School, Wellingborough

The Wonder Of Friends

One is a life-saver,
She's there for a rant.
I can talk to her forever,
Even when I'm under the weather.

Another's smart
And very good at art.
Without her
I feel empty.

The third is a laugh,
Always up for a joke
And never too serious.

And then there's the last,
I love her with all my heart.
Priya's her name,
Always up for a game
Of football and a laugh.

Keri Bounds (12)
Sir Christopher Hatton School, Wellingborough

My PSP

What matters to me,
My PSP because you can't just leave it on the side,
You become a part of it, hearing the crowd scream.
When you score the winning goal, or win the grand prix.
Just the sound of the crowd makes you feel like you are really there,
You have actually won,
Until you turn around
And you're just sitting on a chair, playing a game.

Shane Parmar (12)
Sir Christopher Hatton School, Wellingborough

School Day

I wake up in the morning feeling very, very rough.
Looking forward to my lesson which is very, very tough.
I get ready for school like lightning speed,
But then I forget my breakfast which I really do need.
I walk up to school in the freezing cold.
I may have an umbrella and I hope it doesn't fold.
When I get to school all my friends greet me,
Then we go to our lessons (yawn!)
By the end of the day I'm very tired.
When I get home I lie down
And watch the telly looking like a clown.

Lauren Wenham [11]
Sir Christopher Hatton School, Wellingborough

My Beanbag And Me

Tick-tock, tick-tock,
Still looking at the time.
Sitting on my beanbag,
Listening to the clock chime.

I wait to watch TV,
But it's only half four.
Thinking to myself,
How slow can time go?

I hate having to wait,
It really doesn't help.
Yet my beanbag keeps me patient,
Safe away from a yelp.

The comfy chair's the best,
No need for a test,
My beanbag and me.

Jananie Nikawala [11]
Sir Christopher Hatton School, Wellingborough

Books Are Important To Me

I sit on a shelf,
All by myself.
They pick me up and put me down,
It's very rare I ever get found.
Just 'cause my cover is dull and boring,
When people pick me up it's enough to set them snoring.
Hundreds of years I've sat here all day,
It's hard to keep my boredom at bay.
For pick me up and bang me about,
The librarian gets angry, she gives them a shout,
But someday I know,
It will be friend who picks me up not foe.

Paige Fitzsimmons (11)
Sir Christopher Hatton School, Wellingborough

The Fish That Got Away!

There's nothing more that I like,
Than catching a great big pike,
I cast my float,
From my little boat
And when I get a bite,
I jump up in fright,
Then reel him in with all my might,
Keeping my line nice and tight.

Twisting and turning
My muscles burning
And suddenly, *snap!*
Oh *crap!*
There's been a mishap.

Hayden James (13)
Sir Christopher Hatton School, Wellingborough

What Matters To Me

Sleep is what matters to me
I like to sleep easily
It's what I do when I go to bed
I lie down and rest my head.

I like to dream with a teddy
When my mum says, 'Turn off the telly!'
When I hear water go drip
I stand up and bite my lip.

I stand over my cat
And fall, *splat!*
Into the primary school
Where I used to drool.

My old teacher Mrs Mura
Said, 'You didn't do your homework, did you?'
I ran and stopped
An idea just popped.

I can step out this nightmare
That I'm well aware
I think of my friends
There the love never ends.

Monika, Nicole, Kelsey and Tiffany
I know that's not many
But they're my best friends
And that's what matters to me.

Jacqui Sadler [13]
Sir Christopher Hatton School, Wellingborough

Poverty Is Now

Why on this Earth do we have everything
When loads of people out there,
Have nothing?
When we are lucky to have an education,
When they can't have none?
You've seen them everywhere,
On TV and bus stops,
Billboards and papers.
If they're so noticed,
Why can't people help?
Crying, sobbing for their family,
Thinking that they have no hope,
When actually they do,
Because of us.
Poverty is not just important to me,
It's important to everyone.
So help them today,
Don't let poverty take over.

Samiha Begum (11)
Sir Christopher Hatton School, Wellingborough

My Family

My brother, my brother, can be annoying,
But sometimes can be very interesting.
Usually he'd play with his toys,
Which also can be very interesting.

My mum, my mum, can be helpful,
But sometimes she is very stressful.
Usually she'd do the washing up,
Then cuddle up and watch EastEnders.

My dad, my dad, can be queer,
But also can be very clever.
Usually he'd watch a lot of fishing,
In the garden he'd do a lot of digging.

My family, my family, can be really nice,
But sometimes feels like we are in a cold block of ice.
Usually we'd get together
And watch a lot of TV.

Lewis Turner (11)
Sir Christopher Hatton School, Wellingborough

What Matters To Me!

So, what matters to me,
It must be,
Playing on a Nintendo Wii.
I don't have one,
But when my friend is not gone,
I will ask him like a happy Larry.

The other thing that matters to me,
Is money,
£50, £20, £10, £5 or even £1.
I love money but,
It is so sad when
It has to go in a bank.

The last thing that matters to me,
Must be,
Uuuhhh . . .
That's it,
The last thing that matters to me,
Is my family . . .

Callum Hillman (11)
Sir Christopher Hatton School, Wellingborough

140

Boys, Boys, Boys

Boys, boys, boys
Them and their toys
Boys, boys, boys
And what they enjoy

Boys, boys, boys
I like boys in cars
Boys, boys, boys
I like boys in bars

Boys, boys, boys
I love them
Boys, boys, boys
I am their gem

Boys, boys, boys
I like them with brown eyes
Boys, boys, boys
I like them without ties.

Gemma White (13)
Sir Christopher Hatton School, Wellingborough

Basketball

What matters to me most of all,
Is playing basketball,
Basketball is my favourite sport,
I dribble up and down the court,
All my friends and family,
Cheering me on, supporting me,
The best shot is the slam dunk,
It burns off all that junk,
Swoosh! In it goes,
Then we look at our score as it grows,
I'll get a three-pointer in the net,
The ball flies in the air like a jet,
I've had my shot,
Now it's your turn to take the spot,
But no one can beat me,
You'll see,
I never lose,
Especially with these shoes,
We wear jersey and shorts,
While running around in the courts,
That's our fashion
And basketball is our passion,
All the way to the end,
While the other team just pretend,
We win the cup
And always look up!

Priya Parekh (13)
Sir Christopher Hatton School, Wellingborough

The Drama Of The Last Ball

On a glorious summer's day
A game of cricket I love to play.
Bowled, caught, run out,
Three dreaded ways to get out.
Leg before wicket,
Another way to get out in cricket.
With a good score posted on the board
The opponents know runs need to be scored.
Now with the ball in my possession
I'm looking to bowl a really good session.
Bang! Boom! The runs keep flowing,
They never stop. They just keep flowing,
They never stop. They just keep going.
However I pick up some wickets on the way,
This could turn out to be a good day.
I stand on my mark in my cream white clothes.
As the game draws to a close
We are in the best position.
Surely, no way back for the opposition.
One ball left and two runs to win
With the ball, I start to run in.
Ping! The ball hits the bat,
Only for the keeper to leap like a cat.
He holds on to a spectacular catch.
What a way to end a great match!
The ultimate drama of the last ball
A moment for everyone to recall.

Lewis Kain (13)
Sir Christopher Hatton School, Wellingborough

What Matters To Me . . .

What matters to me
Are all of my family,
They are always there for me
Through good times or through hard times,
I do not care when,
As long as they're there
And to be like my friend.

What matters to me
Are all of my friends at school,
Although we have our ups and downs
We would never be as far apart from the school hall,
My best friends are: Louie, Jacob, Monika, Kelsey and of course - Jacqui!
Even though they're wacky
They all matter to me.

What matters to me
Is my education,
From writing poems with Mrs Lawson
To playing netball with Mrs Reid,
I do not care when I have the lesson,
As long as I succeed!

What matters to me
Is what I eat,
From popping candy that goes *bang* in my mouth,
Or lovely juicy pies,
I do not care what I eat,
As long as it does not get on my clip-on tie!

What matters to me
Are all of my memories,
My good ones,
Or my bad ones,
They are kept safely in my heart
And they will never ever depart.

What matters to me
Is my future,
I do not know what will happen,
But I hope it will be like the world,
That it never ends,
Or even like a roller coaster,
It is just the same as life,
It makes everyone happy,
Unlike changing a baby's nappy.

What matters to me
Is getting into university,
I will need good grades
And will need to study hard,
But that does not bother me,
I can do what I do best
And that is just to be *me.*

What matters to me
Is getting a good job,
I can be a builder
Just like Bob,
Or maybe a swimming teacher
And watch all the children go,
Splash! Splash! Drip! Drip!
But is that what I want to be?
I do not know yet,
It is still a while to go,
For now, I think I just want to be . . .
Free!

Tiffany Ho (13)
Sir Christopher Hatton School, Wellingborough

What Matters To Me!

What matters to me!
Holidays are awesome.
Although I love my friends, my family are the best!
Tae Kwon Do is the best, better than the rest!

My friendship goes up, never down.
All my life I have had a spot for wildlife and animals.
Time also matters to me, time with my friends and family.
Telling the truth, never lie.
Everything I do matters to me.
Remembering my grandad, he matters too!
Small things, big things, anything matters to me.

The only way to get a good grade is to study, study and study.
Only the best grade will get me the job I want/need!

Music and martial arts matter to me.
Everybody matters to me!

Bethany Ellul (13)
Sir Christopher Hatton School, Wellingborough

Little, Little Niece Or Nephew

Little, little niece or nephew
I can't wait to see you

Little, little niece or nephew
I will take you to the zoo
To see your first kangaroo

Little, little niece or nephew
There's a massive queue
To come greet you

Little, little niece or nephew
I will always love you
No matter what you do.

Sophie Lake (13)
Sir Christopher Hatton School, Wellingborough

Basketball

Sport is the best,
I'm wearing a thick vest
But I don't care, cos I look like the rest.
I weave in and out the players
Although I'm dressed in layers
I'm still too light for the weighers
I'm here
And then there
A slamdunker over there!
Miami Heats
Fill the seats
My mind thinks of sweets
Swish!
I've finally caught the fish
Now it's time to plate the dish
The victory is ours
Tick-tock goes the hours
I guess I never needed the powers!

Nicole King (13)
Sir Christopher Hatton School, Wellingborough

Life Cycle

Eventually everyone turns into dust
Our hearts into sand and our blood into rust
Our brains to mush and our bones to marrow
To be fed on by worms, which are fed on by sparrows

Only in youth we truly are free
To love and to laugh and to play and to be
Then we must learn to conform to a school
Where teachers and lessons and uniforms rule

I'm left to wondering if really, it's fair
To subject all childhood to the tedium there
But part of me thinks that truly, it's good
That if learning they crave, then learn it they should

Chemistry, history, maths and the like
Equations and atoms and unearthing the Reich
So when they are older they get a career
Which allows them to be somewhere other than here

On a beach in the sand in Miami perhaps
Or a mountain in Sweden with the snow in their caps
Or maybe a marriage and children they crave
Who will grow and be cared for and of course - misbehave!

Their childhoods depend on your GCSEs
And A-levels and success at all kinds of degrees
At least, you are told this while you're a youth
But when you are older you uncover the truth:

They depend on your loving and nurture and care
(And the occasional fiver, here and there)
They empty your pockets and give you all blame
But you find you don't care; you love them the same

As they get older, they move on and move out
To discover the world and see what's about
You weep a little, but feel happiness too
And feel all their joys as if they happen to you

Life's not all fun; there's balance as well
In murders and madness and pathways to Hell
Ignore the bad times, they do not exist
The past is the past, the now is the bliss

The purpose of this poem, I suppose you could say
Is to love all those close and enjoy every day
Because when the clocks go forward and you become old
Lost all your teeth and are covered in mould
When I ask you the question 'Was your life worth it?'
I expect you to answer 'Of course, it was perfect!'

Jessica Dewdney (16)
South Bromsgrove High School, Bromsgrove

My Brother

Today it's my brother's birthday
It is his special time.
I wish him lots of birthday cheer,
On this sunny day.

I think he looks cool,
His clothes make me drool
And when he's doing bad on COD
I help him level up.

He got £50 today,
I'm gonna steal it now.
But when he figures it is gone
He'll hit me round and round.

Richard Cole (14)
The Priory Ruskin Academy, Grantham

Me And My Grandad

Me and my grandad are cool,
But my grandad can be a bit of a fool.
We go out motor cross racing
And always come back aching.
My grandad's awesome, but my dad I never see.
My grandad I always see. It seems to be.
I would do anything for him,
Because he is a bit dim.
I love my grandad and he loves me,
It still seems to be.

Brandon Smith (12)
The Priory Ruskin Academy, Grantham

Christmas

Today is Christmas time again
There are presents all around the tree
Time to have a pantomime
And play with our new Wii

We are all playing with our new toys
While sat around the fire
Loving all the laughs and joy
And putting out some fliers

Eating all the Christmas pud
And setting the tree alight
Wondering why it looked like mud
While eating Dairylea Lite.

Kristofer Hoyes & Joshua Treadwell (12)
The Priory Ruskin Academy, Grantham

Rain

Rain falling on the floor,
Bouncing up, hitting windows,
Getting sucked, down the drain,
Thunder, lightning, goes the rain,
Lighting up with sparks of light,
Rain bouncing with fear,
People running for shelter in horror,
Flooding streets with boats too!
Rescuing people on lifeboats,
Helicopters hovering over flooding streets,
People in need, hoping for luck.

Nathan Daves (11)
The Priory Ruskin Academy, Grantham

Music

Music is a lot to me,
I like to know the lyrics of Tinie T.
Listening to his songs makes me believe . . .
That sometimes stars look at me.

I also like Eminem,
He's like the character from M and M's.
He could be red, green or blue,
But it doesn't matter he is still cool.

Music makes me feel better,
When I put on my navy blue sweater.
When I go to school,
People don't think of me as a fool,
Because I listen to artists that fill my head up to full.

Waking up in the morning,
Dressing up for school and once again
My iPod is turned up
So I'm ready to rule.

Getting on the bus,
It's freezing outside,
Playing my songs . . .
People think I'm hard.

Patryk Lawniczak (13)
The Priory Ruskin Academy, Grantham

What Matters To Me

What matters to me,
Not cricket and rugby.
Football is the best,
They wear shirts not vests.

What matters to me,
Not Manchester and not Tenby.
London is amazing,
Big Ben and the London Eye are astonishing.

What matters to me,
Not Las Vegas and not Washington DC.
New York is awesome,
It is not like eating a plum.

But what matters to me, the best,
Not my toys, not my house, not even my life is the best.
What matters more is my family,
Such as my mum, my dad and my brother especially.

Jonathan Short [11]
The Priory Ruskin Academy, Grantham

Steam Train

Trains, trains puffing down the track,
The faster they go the more they clack.
Rushing past the cows and the sheep,
Listening to the train as it goes peep, peep.

Racing down the line because the signal is down,
Going past the traffic in Grantham town.
Here's the end of the line, looking real fine,
We better get off, because it is time.

James Smith [12]
The Priory Ruskin Academy, Grantham

What Matters To Me?

Animals and habitats
Trees fall with fears
Animals fall with tears
Why does it have to be this way?
They hit the ground like bombs
But don't expect to fall
It doesn't have to be this way.
Animals get shot, pinned down and poached
Whilst their friends watch in hope.

War
Many people are dying
Lots of people are lying,
Both sides fight,
But want to be at home with their children, flying a kite.
Why do we have to fight?
Storming through the desert,
wondering who's over the bank.
They crawl up slowly
Like a lizard in a water tank.
Why do people have to die?

Sam Rose (12)
The Priory Ruskin Academy, Grantham

Winter

Snow falls,
Snowballs thrown,
Children call,
Coldness known.

Christmas comes,
After my birthday,
Presents galore,
For my birthday.

Snowmen tower,
Children gather,
Bullies come round,
Snowmen fall down.

After Christmas
And my birthday,
Comes new year,
After Boxing Day.

So when Christmas comes,
After my birthday,
I know I have more presents,
In a short space of time.

Alex White (13)
The Priory Ruskin Academy, Grantham

Soldier's Mourn

As he lit the fire,
On that cold winter night,
A knock on the door,
Gave him an awful fright.

He jumped to his feet
And he opened the door,
'Sit tight,' he said,
To his girls on the floor.

There stood a man,
In an army outfit,
He knew what was coming,
The guns and the pits.

He sat down with his girls
And he told them the news.
'I'll be gone in the morning.'
He gave them the clues.

'I'm going to war,'
He explained to his wife.
She sobbed and she cried,
'But you might lose your life!'

The night went so fast,
The morning drew near.
As the truck drove away,
He shed a small tear.

Days went by
And he never returned.
'He may be dead,'
His wife and kids learnt.

He'd fought the Germans,
Throughout night and day.
He watched his friends die,
In pain, as they lay.

But one day it was him,
He was shot in the gut,
He thought of his family
And nothing but.

He soon fell asleep,
Alone in the snow,
How awful it was to die
And have nobody know.

As she lit the fire,
On that cold winter night,
A knock on the door,
Gave her an awful fright.

She jumped to her feet
And she opened the door.
'Sit tight,' she said,
To her girls on the floor.

There stood a man
In an army outfit,
She knew what was coming . . .

Matthew Cording (13)
The Priory Ruskin Academy, Grantham

Global Warming

Global warming is an annoying thing.
All you had to do was put it in the bin.
Dumping things in lakes and fields . . .
Rotting cakes and rusty wheels.
Remember when we didn't have to watch what we do?
Or even what we put down the loo?
The world cannot last forever . . .
So treat it well
And don't step on every shell
Because we are all living
So we all deserve to earn a living.

We all make mistakes
But we all deserve a break
From the never-ending ache . . .
The government.

Marcus Kingston [14]
The Priory Ruskin Academy, Grantham

BMX

BMXing, the great feeling you get
When you're in mid-air
Flying through the air
It feels like you're in slow motion
Even though you're really fast
The hilarious moment when you make a stupid mistake
But avoid injury
You and your mates
Laughing and joking
It's not just a skate park
It's a social club.

Kristian Willetts [13]
The Priory Ruskin Academy, Grantham

Boys Are Such A Mystery

You say one thing but mean another,
You flirt and say things you don't mean,
You pretend to care but really don't,
Boys are such a mystery!

You said you love me,
You don't really,
You made me fall for you,
Boys are such a mystery!

Here's a tip,
You will need it!

Don't make a girl fall for you,
If you don't intend on catching her!

Boys are such a mystery!

Hannah Giddens (14)
The Priory Ruskin Academy, Grantham

What Matters To Me

My hobbies are dancing and singing,
It keeps me fit and healthy.
I'm not very confident in front of an audience,
But it makes me feel good.

I love it when new music comes out,
So I can learn the words and sing along.
I love the singers Katy Perry and Shontel,
They have good songs and moves.

I watch the X Factor, but every time I do
I think to myself, *I wish I could be up there too.*

Charmaine Dickson (13)
The Priory Ruskin Academy, Grantham

Best Friends

Best friends are forever,
You should always stay together,
Through thick and thin,
Don't throw your friendship in the bin.
You can have more than one best friend,
They may set the trend.
Friendship makes me feel happy!

Best friends are forever,
Some may not stick together,
Friends always have their ups and downs.
Your friendship may be worth some pounds.
Your best friends may make you feel joyful,
They can also be very thoughtful,
Friendship makes me feel happy!

Emma Collingwood (13)
The Priory Ruskin Academy, Grantham

Halloween Magic

Halloween - time for spooky ghosts and ghouls,
Candles burning inside of creepy pumpkins
And skeletons walking around the streets,
Trick or treats after every last bit of candy.
Scarier zombies rising from their graves.

The werewolves are howling at the full moon,
The mummy is coming out of his coffin in Egypt.
The witches are out to cast a spell on you
And finally the true magic of Halloween comes to life.

Jake Bentley (13)
The Priory Ruskin Academy, Grantham

Skiing

I like skiing,
Over the crisp white snow.
The wind is howling,
It makes my fingers glow!

Turning and twisting on the slopes,
I'm going to get down to the bottom I hope?
Not so, I take a tumble!
That makes me mad,

Because I'm not as good as I thought I was,
But then, it's not too bad?
I straighten up and try again.

I'm nearly at the bottom.
I forget that I am hurt.
I'll try again tomorrow.

Daniel Cook (12)
The Priory Ruskin Academy, Grantham

War

Bullets are shot,
Plans to plot,
Bodies are hit,
Lying in the pit,
It's such a bore,
It's a war!

Conor Ross (12)
The Priory Ruskin Academy, Grantham

War

Many people risk their lives,
But many don't survive.
Children and wives get upset,
But they'll never ever forget.

The problems that get involved
Violence has never ever solved.
We need to communicate
And not stab people in the heart.

Many people risk their lives
But many don't survive.
Their souls disappear
But they don't regret.
All the time they've shared,

Even though they use guns.
In the end, it will get rid of all the fun.
I don't like the way this happens
Every time some break,
A bone in their body, which will ache.

Many people risk their lives
But many don't survive.
The world better prepare,
When I close my eyes
And reveal a horror.

Many people risk their lives
But many don't survive.

Jessica Marshall (14)
The Priory Ruskin Academy, Grantham

My Hand

My hand, my hand
Has let me down
Once again
It's made me frown
I've looked and looked
And what I've found
I've always taken
My hand for granted
Like a blind man
And his dog panting
My hand, my hand
I didn't see it coming
I wasn't prepared
And now I'm suffering.

Charlie Pirie (14)
The Priory Ruskin Academy, Grantham

Recycling

Recycling is important because of the ice
If you don't recycle the only thing you'll see is rubbish and *mice!*

People need to stop cutting down trees
To save the animals, monkeys and bees.

If all the ice melts the polar bears will die
And then Mother Nature will cry.

If we change now, the world will be a better place.
So make sure you recycle, do not waste.

Adam Walker (11)
The Priory Ruskin Academy, Grantham

Homelessness

I'm angry, mad and even sad!
They have no home, nor money or clothes,
Why does no one help them?
Why can't anyone see
All the differences between them and me?

They say that dogs are a man's best friend,
Sit there with no money to spend.
They weep, they sob and they shriek,
All dirty and very weak.

Some people walk by
And turn a blind eye.
Some people stop and say hello,
Some people give them money
But others just say 'no'.

Callum Atkinson (13)
The Priory Ruskin Academy, Grantham

Pets

My cat is lazy
My dog is crazy.
My rabbit is bouncy
My hamster is flouncy.
My fish likes swimming
My bird likes singing.
My horse lives in a stable
My mouse likes a nibble on the cable.
My rat is smelly
My cow has a big belly.

Animals are amazing!

Nathan Jessop (11)
The Priory Ruskin Academy, Grantham

Help For Heroes

Bullets are shot,
Screaming is heard,
Bombs are exploded,
People are killed,
The message gets home,
The fear is still here,
But the hope is always there,
The war still rages on,
The troops who lost their lives,
Their legacy still lives,
But they are gone.

Jack Perry [13]
The Priory Ruskin Academy, Grantham

Halo Reach

Halo Reach is the best
It whoops the rest;
Especially COD,
In campaign it is awesome.
Jorge and Emile plus Carter
Are the coolest in campaign . . .

I may not be the best in matchmaking
But forge I kick butt, I can make an immaculate map
With any game type I play awesomely.

Playing Halo I've made cool screenshots,
Completed the campaign, done epic glitches,
I have epic armour because my level
And my epic maps are great.
I've gotten to Warrant Officer grade 1.

Adam Kimmings [12]
The Priory Ruskin Academy, Grantham

Global Warming

Global warming is a big issue,
If we don't make a contribution we'll have to cover our house with tissues.
Coughs and sneezes will cover our lives
Unless we wait for a miracle or a surprise.

This world is melting and pollution is corrupting.
Put a stop to this problem
Or we'll have no electricity to even ride dodgems.
As we release gases and fuels into the atmosphere
In future we'll have no cars to even change gear.

It could really change our lives
So in future we'll have lots of oil to dive.
Global warming really is a big issue,
Please make a contribution then there'll be no need for tissues.

Poobeash Gomahan (14)
The Priory Ruskin Academy, Grantham

The Win

It was match point,
He served and I returned,
He was strong but so was I,
I wasn't going to give up,
I tried harder, he fought back,
Then I went for a smash,
I had won,
The cheers for me were great,
But this was only a dream.

Carl Jennings (13)
The Priory Ruskin Academy, Grantham

Animal Abuse

When people are angry,
They keep getting cranky,
Releasing their devastation
On the heart of their animals.

Animal abuse is like a wall,
It's mean and tough
And never gets you anywhere.

In the vision of the pets,
It may blind them,
With the fear,
Of being unloved.

Thus being hit
And getting scars,
Think in your heart,
Please help them.

Victor Lima (13)
The Priory Ruskin Academy, Grantham

Pollution

Pollution, it ruins people's lives.
You see it everywhere, all over the floor
Around bins in corners, it's on every street
Just put it in the bin to help people around the world
It will stop animals dying
Pick the litter up before it's too late!

Toby Bonnefin (13)
The Priory Ruskin Academy, Grantham

When Our Loves Go To War

When our loves go to war
There's machines, guns and all things more.
All we know, the end may near
With the nightmare noises we hear.

The crashes and bangs
Then the telephones rang,
So mothers cry and children sob,
Who can stop this shooting mob?

You've seen them laugh, you've seen them cry,
Now let's just hope they won't die.

Come on now please, I beg you all
Let's all stop this shooting freefall.

Full stop!

Tia Jade Sculthorpe (13)
The Priory Ruskin Academy, Grantham

Judo

Hearing my name called out
Raring to go
Tension building, adrenaline racing
Ready to fight
Raring to go
Referee calls, 'Go.'
Can't go back now
Coach screaming, mind leaping
To go for the throw
I've gone and won
Smiling and opponent crying
Waiting for the next rival.

Brennan Knight (13)
The Priory Ruskin Academy, Grantham

War

People suffering everywhere,
We're acting like we just don't care,
But this war has already begun,
And all the dangers from the barrel of a gun.

Lots of danger in the open plains,
Where it's hot and never rains,
But this war is never done,
And all the dangers from the barrel of a gun.

Stop the flights; stop the war,
Make the battling against the law,
Civilisation's existence is on the brink,
Just take a second to stop and think.

This isn't the way to win the fight,
Just have a go to make it right,
Civilisation's existence is down the sink,
Just a second to stop and think.

Connor Brown (12)
The Priory Ruskin Academy, Grantham

Friends

My friends make me happy
My friends make me laugh
Some of them are wappy
Some of them are daft
They give me advice
It shows they care
We chat and play all day
And sweets we share
We fight then make up again
Because we have things in common
My friends make me happy.

Keenan Leeton (13)
The Priory Ruskin Academy, Grantham

The Other Side

On the other side I will be
Waiting until you are here with me.
Oh how I long to hold your hand
And walk across a beach of golden sand.

The other side is really great
It's something even you could not hate.
All I ask is for you not to grieve
As I will never leave.
I will always be in your heart
So that the feelings we feel will never part.

When the day comes for you to go
Please don't feel really low.
Because death is a wonderful thing
Think of all the happiness it will bring.

I will see you soon my dear
Just remember that I'm always here.
We were made for each other
As you were such a good lover.
I look down at you to see your face
It always lights up with grace.

So please do not grieve
As I will never leave.
You will always be in my heart
Because the love I felt for you will always be in my heart.

On the other side I will be
Waiting until you're here with me.

Jake Weston [13]
The Priory Ruskin Academy, Grantham

My Poem

Everyday life is what I like.
Chilling out is what I do.
Keeping up with the latest things.
Looking nice with my new clothes.
Buying new things is what I do
And that's how I roll.

Being kind and trustworthy,
Helping out with jobs.
Being reliable and responsible.
Looking out for people.
Looking after people I care about.
Being polite and having manners.
Knowing people love me.
Appreciating what people do for me
And that's how I roll.

Aaron Redhead (12)
The Priory Ruskin Academy, Grantham

Family

Mums and dads are always there
They are always there to care.
Mums and dads give you treats
But only seven days a week.

My mum and dad are just the best
I think they deserve a rest.
Brothers and sisters always fight
You really need to say goodnight.

My mum and dad always have a good plan
When we go and see my old gran.
I love my family very much
I think we should stay in touch.

Matthew Collingwood (12)
The Priory Ruskin Academy, Grantham

Fireflies

Fireflies hide in tall trees
Silently chase away darkness
A flash here
A sparkle there
Too fast to pinpoint
They dance here
And shine there
Destroying the darkness of our mind

Soon they come
With a glowing shine
They get brighter, soon the time will come
Now the days get brighter
Their shine is disappearing

Now it comes
The days are brighter
The fireflies soon disappear
No more sparkle
No more shine
The night is getting here
The last few sparkles disappear
Darkness grows upon us
No more fireflies
People wearily wait for them
Not sure if they will return
Then!
A flash here
A sparkle there
The night grows brighter
They are back and here to stay.

Thomas Baker (13)
The Priory Ruskin Academy, Grantham

Sport

I like swimming, I think it's pretty cool.
The best bit is when you jump in the pool.
The worst bit is when your trunks fall down.
It makes you want to drown.

I quite like tennis.
I think it is the best.
The only thing I lose to the rest
But I can beat my guest.

Ben Musson (13)
The Priory Ruskin Academy, Grantham

Snowboarding

I put my boots on
And wait in line
For the train to the top
Get on the train
Go to the top
Climb on my board, when there
The wind blowing, snow falling
The sight getting less and less
Off I go
Down and down
Weaving in and out of people
My brother falls off a lot
I go over a jump higher, higher
As I land some idiot goes past
Pushing my brother over, I abuse him
Take him out, laughing he falls
My dad abuses him and stops, he calls us idiots
Rides off, yet laughing still, we make
Our way to the bottom
And off we go again.

Ryan Smith (13)
The Priory Ruskin Academy, Grantham

Who Am I?

Being busy is what I do best,
From making a mess,
To causing great stress.

Standing in line to see the headmaster,
Do I run now or will he be faster?

I like who I am,
I don't know any better,
As long as I've got love, life and laughter.
I wouldn't want to be any other.

Happy and proud
To be me?

Who am I?
I'm what you see!

Thomas Kendall (13)
The Priory Ruskin Academy, Grantham

My Family

My mum is lovely and beautiful like a rose petal.
She does everything for me.
My cousin is a cutie, he is a 1-year-old.
My grandad is nice like a butterfly, he makes me laugh all the time.
My grandma is cool, she is funny like my grandad, they are both nice.

Inga Swiderek (13)
The Priory Ruskin Academy, Grantham

Killer

Waiting round the back door,
A killer stands with no affection at all.

Sorrow faces crying in pain,
Whilst forced to sit on chairs of shame.

A man stands stiff and tall,
Waiting for the moment to leg out the front door.

Neighbours hear a scream and a bang
And a slam of the door, then the telephone rang.

Nee-naw, nee-naw,
Cars rush down,
Crying and screaming comes from the crowd.

Dead bodies are rolled to the car near the door,
Killer not found,
No happiness at all.

Ellie White (13)
The Priory Ruskin Academy, Grantham

War At Afghan

People dying,
Bullets flying,
The world is now fighting,
Over things that don't need to be fought,
Young people dying for their country,
Blood splattering,
Dead people lying,
Soldiers lose their friends and start crying,
People dying,
Bullets flying,
People crying.

Bradley Butterworth (13)
The Priory Ruskin Academy, Grantham

Poverty

The world around us is a bad place,
For the people who have no space,
To live and move or even breathe,
In this world it's a squeeze.

People who have no money often end up without,
These people are without a doubt the poorest people about,
They cannot shout, they have no time,
They have to live in the dirt,
Without so much as a shirt.

Big governments ignore these people,
They pretend they don't exist,
These people always have to try
To do their best to survive.

No matter where these people live,
Poverty can be relative,
They cry, they scream, they even shout,
But we don't hear them,
We don't care,
For it's a truth we can't even bear.

So we ignore them when they're there
And we judge them when they're not,
But let me ask you one last thing and it will answer everything,
Do you really even care when they sit and just stare?

Samuel Acklam (14)
The Priory Ruskin Academy, Grantham

The White Rhino

The white rhino,
Big, majestic and strong,
All of those ugly hunters,
Hunting in the wrong.

A big game rifle,
The bullet from a gun,
To the hunters a mere trifle,
The slaughter has begun.

Shooting all the wildlife,
Making such a bungle,
Pursuing in the deserts
And hunting in the jungle.

Still following a sport,
Long outdated,
Still hunting rhinos,
The armour plated.

For hunters it's a game,
Blasting with their gun,
For rhinos it's a shame,
For hunters it's just fun.

Becoming extinct,
A terrible loss for us,
The end of the great and mighty,
Majestic rhinoceros.

Luke George David Cox (14)
The Priory Ruskin Academy, Grantham

I Wanna Be A Star

I like football
I wanna be a star,
I like lots of sports
But rugby might take me far.

I like computers
Particularly the games,
If I carry on
It will start to help my brains.

I like my family
And my friends,
I hope this happiness
Never ends.

I like the Academy,
I think it's the best school,
The teachers are great
And the lessons are cool!

Oliver Buchan-Papworth (11)
The Priory Ruskin Academy, Grantham

Miners

M y husband is one of those men stuck,
　　stuck down that deep, dark hole.
 I wait for him to get out to, to escape from that deep, dark hole.
N iko is his name, waiting is his game,
　　waiting to get out of that deep, dark hole.
E mpty is his heart, empty is his soul,
　　empty is his soul, empty because of that deep, dark hole.
R eading cannot be done, neither can escaping,
　　escaping from that deep, dark hole.
S till we are waiting, no signs of escaping,
　　escaping from that deep, dark hole.

Nathan Walker (12)
The Priory Ruskin Academy, Grantham

Things That Matter To Me

Many things matter to me,
I am going to state just three,
First I will talk about,
Global warming without a doubt.

The heat is making the ice caps melt,
I have got to tighten my belt,
Now I'm going to talk about,
Family that make me scream and shout.

Family have a lot of fun,
Me, my dad, my sisters and my mum,
We all live in our little house,
Me, my sister, my dad and his spouse.

Finally I am going to say,
Something that may brighten your day,
The final thing that matters to me,
Is the Earth, the land and sea.

Robert Durham (13)
The Priory Ruskin Academy, Grantham

Young Writers Information

We hope you have enjoyed reading this
book - and that you will continue to enjoy it
in the coming years.

If you like reading and writing poetry drop
us a line, or give us a call, and we'll send
you a free information pack.

Alternatively if you would like to order further
copies of this book or any of our other titles,
then please give us a call or log onto our
website at www.youngwriters.co.uk

Young Writers Information
Remus House
Coltsfoot Drive
Peterborough
PE2 9BF
(01733) 890066